TREKKING

TREKKING

In Search of the Real South Africa

Denis Beckett

PENGUIN BOOKS

PENGUIN BOOKS

Published by the Penguin Group
27 Wrights Lane, London W8 5TZ, England
Viking Penguin, a division of Penguin Books USA Inc, 375 Hudson Street,
New York, New York 10014, USA
Penguin Books Australia Ltd, Ringwood, Victoria, Australia
Penguin Books Canada Ltd, 10 Alcorn Avenue, Toronto, Ontario, Canada
M4V 3B2
Penguin Books (NZ) Ltd, 182-190 Wairau Road, Auckland 10, New
Zealand
Penguin Books South Africa (Pty) Ltd, Pallinghurst Road, Parktown, South
Africa 2193

Penguin Books South Africa (Pty) Ltd, Registered Offices: 20 Woodlands
Drive, Woodmead, Sandton, South Africa 2128

First published by Penguin Books South Africa (Pty) Ltd 1996

ISBN 0 140 26481 7

Typeset in 10.5 on 13.5 point Life
by Iskova Image Setting
Printed and bound by Interpak Natal

Contents

Overture

There is a great beauty attached to this book. Namely, that there is no need to start at the beginning or end at the end.

For people I know or might yet know, there is also a great relief. I hereby declare that not a single soul need ever feel that sinking feeling: 'Um, hasn't he written some sort of book, I'd better say something nice about it.' Be at liberty to dismiss it, ignore it, or free-read a chunk in the bookshop and then shove it back on the shelf.

A TV show does terrible things to human relationships: 'Um, doesn't he do some sort of TV programme, I'd better sound polite about it.' Nobody needs to think that. A media person who expects everybody to watch his show, read his book, whatever, deserves what he gets, namely disillusionment.

I, the flesh-and-blood human being who eats lunches, carries supermarket parcels to the parking lot, and takes kids to school, am not the figure who wafts through the airwaves into the unsuspecting living room.

That guy, you do things to that you would never do to me or any real person. You yell at him: 'Shurrup!' or 'Rubbish!' or 'What's this junk!'. You slam your finger on him, shutting him out more instantly than you shoo a stray cat from the kitchen.

Then I bump into you in the cinema queue and you feel embarrassed, as if caught committing a hypocrisy.

Relax. The media figure is a figment, a distortion, a virtual person. The real person is the one whose presence is precisely as real to you as yours is to him.

Divorce the two. Insult the guy on the screen to your heart's content, and feel no guilt when you encounter his alter ego. Relate to the living breathing human as you relate to any other.

This book is about the TV series Beckett's Trek. It describes some of the experiences that arose from spending fourteen months and a tanker-load of petrol wandering the highways and byways in search of South Africa. It is littered with asides and irrelevancies and opinionations. Also with social and quasi-political perspectives which, my publisher Alison Lowry tells me I should warn you in advance, are apt to come across as perplexing in that they range from 'Right' to 'Left' and are sometimes both at the same time.

This may appear inconsistent, but it is not an inconsistency I apologise for. Rather the opposite, in fact. These simplistic categories 'Right' and 'Left' are now meaningless hangovers from a past era.

The quest in my mind is straightforward. It is for a South Africa that delivers prosperity and contentment, and a sense of being at home, being at ease, being secure, across the board.

I have no interest in finding comfort for any one segment at the expense of discomfort for any other. I seek a society where whether I am in Sandton or Rosettenville or Wonderboom or Athlone or Guguletu or Verulam or Smithfield I find a prevailing attitude that says 'we're on top of things, we're moving forward, we're confident'. At present I do not see that attitude prevailing in any of those quarters.

To acquire it, I have no doubt that a new spectrum of thought is necessary. I suspect that this new spectrum is now being born, albeit a bit long in the gestation, and that with its birth the bulk of historical ideologies, 'Right' and 'Left' and a good deal of what is inbetween, will be consigned to the dustbin.

While the book is more of a joll than a political direction-finder, certain observations in respect of the vraagstukke do creep in. To the extent that they feature they belong in the new and inchoate spectrum rather than the old and sterile one. (Okay, Alison?)

1
Murphy's Law

The SABC was in Acting mode in 1994.
Practically everybody was Acting, from
Acting Assistant Soundman to Acting General
Manager. The idea was to have slots on
hand to accommodate the advance guard of
black incomers, but the idea failed to pay
due care and attention to the Law of
Unintended Consequences, a.k.a. Murphy's.

With the executive offices half populated
by Affirmatives desperately feeling around
for the ropes and half by precarious Old
Guarders terrified of attracting attention,
finding a decision in the building was like
finding someone who admitted to having
supported apartheid. And when a decision
did take place, the results were apt to be
otherwise. There was for instance the Great
Leap Forward, when to supercharge the
pace of change volunteer retrenchees were
called for.

There was no shortage of response, but
more than half was from black applicants.
In vain did the Human Resources mense
explain: 'No, the *whites* quit, so you guys
can move up.' Indignant blacks and their

shop stewards threatened to sue for discrimination, and several of the corporation's prize black blue-eyed boys ended up sailing into the sunset happily counting their packages.

It was boom time for perversity, but from my personal perspective one perversity eclipsed all the others. Because of two consecutive affirmative action appointments, I, male and pale and supposedly a prime victim of the process, wound up with the kind of job you expect to get only from genies or fairy godmothers.

Step 1 was in March '94. I got a call from Zweli Mncube, Acting Economics Editor. I didn't know Zweli and was intrigued that he wanted an 'urgent, urgent' meeting, over lunch if possible. That sounded fine, and we sat in the new Yard restaurant, formerly the Yard Of Ale but recently bought over by a black consortium who dropped the Of and the Ale to mark the occasion.

Zweli wanted me to host – starting immediately – a weekly talkshow called Face the Fax, on NNTV. I had never heard of this show, and had only dimly heard of NNTV, which, like most South Africans, I assumed was some leftover or experimental channel that had nothing to do with me. After all, until recently its name had been 'Top Sport Surplus' channel, which must have been offputting even for sports freaks, let alone the rest of us.

Anycase, TV talkshowing was by no means my line. I had, to be true, done a bit of it over the last year. There was a show called Slabbert on Sunday and on three occasions, when Van Zyl Slabbert was away, I had been Acting Slabbert. I had done these for the simple reason that I could use the pay, but after each one I had been more conscious than before of the heaviness of the going. For an unremitting hour you're trying to sustain lively debate on matters such as rural development policy options. Uh oh.

So I was hardly keen. But Zweli insisted that this one was jam. It would be exactly like my radio talkshow, he said, except I'd get home earlier. It wound up at 10.45 instead of midnight.

My first doubt was that Zweli was missing the point, and I said so. The SABC hadn't employed him to hide his about-to-be-enfranchised face in a back room. They wanted him on camera. Zweli said yes, he knew that, and had done his best to oblige, but for hours and nights before he had to appear on camera he couldn't sleep, couldn't think, his bodily functions were all messed up, it was no go.

I knew that feeling, all right. In fact I also knew about the sleepless nights of *after* a media appearance. These were the nights that got consumed with thinking up all the brilliant ripostes you would have given this caller or that comment if only you'd thought them up in time. These were the nights of mortification over that which you had said but ought to have left unsaid and frustration over that which you had left unsaid but ought to have said. The post-performance night was a night of bad memories and the pre-performance night was a night of bad anticipation, frantically trying to sleep so as to be rested and relaxed with brain attuned for the ordeal ahead, and hearing the clock chime 12, and then 1, and 2, and 3 . . .

I could see Zweli's point. What I couldn't see was why I wanted to lose any more of my own sleep. Perhaps it was that my so-called 'career' − obnoxious word − was not going any particular place in terms of the print media which had always been my first love. Perhaps it was that I was slowly acquiring a taste for TV's cousin radio, where I was into my third year of a weekly 3-hour show on the dominant talk-station 702. Perhaps it was the outlandishness of the idea − Zweli wanted me to focus on economic issues, which was hilarious for a guy who barely knew a bank rate from a foreign reserve. Perhaps it was that Zweli was so desperate, and so nice. Perhaps it was that TV was paying about twice as much for 45 minutes as radio was for three hours or newspapers for eight. Whatever, I agreed to face faxes until Zweli could find a permanent occupant.

After two weeks I was wanting out. This thing was awful. Each minute was eternity before an unrelenting live camera −

actually four unrelenting cameras — while a vast flow of written questions crossed my lap and a small number of business experts explained subjects about which I did not understand even the vocabulary.

But Zweli kept persuading me to help out for one more week, one more week, and then all of a sudden — not a warning word — Zweli was gone, following his predecessor Alec Hogg (also the first fax-facer) to Absa bank.

The new Acting Economics Ed was another Affirmative Action appointment, Tanya Glavovic. If they couldn't find a dark body at least they could find a female one, which was a slightly poor second but a second nonetheless. Moreover, Tanya was pretty much up on money matters. Just that she was not cut out for an exec role. (Her Acting regency lasted a whole couple of years after which they reverted, in the person of Reg Rumney, to the dreaded white male once again.)

Tanya made it amply clear that she had enough problems without expending energy on this remote and unwanted corner of her empire, and she certainly had no time to worry about a presenter replacement. Funnily enough this became another reason that the weeks stretched on into months and the months multiplied. If I'd quit it would have dropped the show's wonderful director, Marie Minnaar, splat in the soup. Not even a presenter's nightmare is as nightmarish as a director's nightmare of pitching up on Tuesday night with lights and cameras and guests and an empty chair next to the fax machine.

So I stayed, I stayed, and bit by bit warmed to the task. Even as it lost its terrors, though, it still meant that I was wiping out all of Tuesday night and much of the day. You might say 'but it was only 45 minutes', and yes, so it was, but that ignores hype-up time and wind-down time and research time and organisation time and snoop-about time to find out which guests would avoid making the viewer's screen implode with boredom.

We hit jackpot now and again, such as with Pierre du Toit, the world's most entertaining tax accountant, but there were times there, as in detailing the distinctions between Phases III and IV of the Motor Industry Rationalisation Programme, that I thought we might be sued for unfair competition by the insomnia-cure industry.

Notwithstanding, I acquired almost a fondness for my fax machine, and I will make at least one claim for the programme, which is that it became a million miles more accessible to the man in the street than any economics show before or since. In fact it was the only economics show I ever heard of that the man in the street could begin to follow, being the only economics programme ever hosted by the man in the street.

Discussion was often on a really basic level. Once I had Chris Liebenberg, Minister of Finance, going on about deficits, debt, and debt traps. I gulped, apologised for my shortcomings, and asked him to explain the difference between deficit and debt. Chris was his normal obliging self but he must have suspected he'd been caught in a kindergarten. I felt secretly rather red-faced until the next day when began a months-long flow of people saying 'thank heavens — I also never knew'.

Additionally there was an uncommon quota of fun and games. The fax machine was on set, the star of the show, and people were constantly faxing forth caustic comments about my clothes, hair, adam's apple and whathaveyou, and sometimes about the guests as well. I would read these epistles out if they were short enough and legible — the bane of the show was long handwritten faxes which I was supposed to master at the same time as directing the discussion. The snotty cracks were often the high points. In the middle of some lengthy account of the new formula for phasing out textile tariffs I'd get a fax criticising my tie. The things that echoed, that got remembered and commented upon, had less to do with the tariff formulae than the ties.

With a sum total of one exception, public use of this vehicle of communication was basically decent. I use 'basically' advisedly, as the cracks about my appearance sometimes cut

5

the decencies rather fine, but only one single citizen of South Africa ever totally disgraced himself or the rest of us. That night one of the guests was a black American, a director of affirmative action for Ford, a lovely gentlemanly guy whose answers were not always especially pointed or relevant to SA circumstances. Some sonuvabitch wrote out in large koki letters a list of the worst American (maybe he wasn't a citizen of SA after all) slang insults for black people, and sent it in obviously hoping that the camera would pick it up rolling off the fax. By the grace of God I happened to glance at it just as the first word came up, and I obscured it pronto. The Sunday Times didn't get an International Incident, but the Ford fellow noticed, and I felt terrible. It threw him right off his stroke.

Given that as economics programmes go the Fax was in many ways an ultimate People's economics, it was something of a shock to hear, early in '95, that the new sources of power had adjudged the programme 'elitist', that sole word worse than 'racist'.

I only heard of this condemnation by accident, which was par for the course. I only heard anything by accident. This one happened because I had just heard, by accident, that two months previously the budget had been changed from R125 a minute to R1 000 a minute.

I was flummoxed as to how the overtime bill for the handful of staff could add up to R45 000, but perceived that an 800% increase ought to mean that we could spruce up the set and maybe glamorise the programme elsewise as well. I set out to enquire, and was advised: 'Not to worry, it's an elitist programme so it's coming off sometime soon, around mid-year.'

This view was held evidently by the new head of TV, Solly Mokhehle, and his new No 2 Joe Thloloe, an ex-newspaper type and former subordinate of my former subordinate Aggrey Klaaste but now occupying a broadcasting rank of such dizzy height that I never set eyes on him in the premises. When word got around of the 'elitist' it was mainly met with ribald criticism, but I had a sneaking sympathy with what Solly and Joe were getting at. Not that I *knew* what they were getting at, y'understand, being a mere lowly presenter bobbing like a cork upon a sea of executive deliberation. But I *assumed* that their worry was the name, and I could see why. The name implied that the programme was for people who had faxes at home, which cut out 99,99% of the newly enfranchised.

Actually, the name was misleading as people could, and did, phone in as well (to a reception team outside the studio who sent me a précis), but 'Face the Phone' wouldn't have sounded right at all. I suppose that when the show started, a year before Zweli's SOS, there had been a positive attached to the up-market innuendo. The same positive would later creep back again through advertising strategy documents, but early '95 was not its moment.

So I didn't squawk overly about the impending axe, and awaited its delivery with equanimity. Sooner or later, I assumed, they would determine a wind-up date and then I could relax on Tuesdays, the soonness or lateness depending primarily on when they worked out what to put in the Fax's place.

A month later this assumption was consolidated at an actual formal meeting. Operating on the instructions descending from on high, Louis Raubenheimer, Acting General Manager of NNTV, and Bob Kearsley, Acting Editor in Chief of Television News Productions, confirmed that FtF was now in its last months, and briefly batted around the question of the replacement.

I was asked, fairly casually, if I had any bright ideas, and I said it seemed to me there was potential in the possibility of a fair-minded but ever-so-slightly maverick look at current affairs through the eyes of a presenter who wouldn't be shy of shouting the odds from time to time instead of being the perpetually detached newsreader.

Louis and Bob wanted to know what did I mean, and not quite knowing what I did mean I said: 'Something like Whicker's World', by which what I actually meant was 'here's a name to latch on, to deflect further enquiry'. I had only seen one Whicker's World once, decades before in Britain, and had no clearer a notion of what it entailed than that it seemed strong on the wry, the tangent, and the unexpected, and had struck me thus as somewhat more vibrant than the customary formula of reams of safe blurry facts.

Bob was anti, Louis was lukewarm, the meeting was ending anyhow, and it didn't matter because all we'd really needed to ascertain was that the Fax would roll on for a diminishing but non-imminent while yet.

In the light of which it was a surprise to get home on a Tuesday afternoon a few weeks later and hear an anonymous voice on my answering machine saying I needn't come in tonight, Face the Fax was herewith cancelled.

On enquiry I discovered that there had been the latest and last in a long line of blow-ups between Tanya, at that stage still Acting Economics Editor and now happily ensconced as (non-Acting!) Economics Consultant, and the NNTV programming department, ending with NNTV inviting her to take toys, cot, programme and all somewhere else.

This I could understand, but I was unimpressed to be given the boot on half a day's notice, through the agency of an unknown functionary within the NNTV administration, via an answering machine, with the proximate cause being a row in which I had no part.

Peeved, I faxed NNTV a sarcastic note to suggest that if this was how they treated the plebs they might as well save on those interminable courses about Human Utilisation and Management Sensitivity that were the rage of the day.

It was a fairly rude missive, designed more to deliver a piqued and pointless death-rattle than to elicit a reply, and having despatched it I mentally closed the book on my foray into TV. I had in any case just started my new magazine, Sidelines, and I was feeling precarious straddling four different brands of media — newspaper, radio, TV, and now quarterly journal. This was goodbye to the SABC, where I had never really belonged anyhow.

But Louis Raubenheimer phoned, very handsomely, to say sorry I'd been offended and, er, by the way, would I care to replace the Fax with something like the idea I'd raised that day with Bob?

Fortuitously Bob, who a month earlier had been King or at any rate Lord High Executioner of the SABC, had meantime disappeared back to Australia and out of the SABC's collective mind with a clanging finality. So he wasn't objecting, and neither was whoever was the latest incarnation of Acting Ed-in-Chief of TNP. I said, sure, when do we start? Louis said: how about next week?

2

The Power of Accident

Here beganneth a new dimension to the concept of 'time' in my life. FtF, whatever tensions it caused by way of prefix and suffix, had been fantastically cheap in respect of on-display time. One minute on camera equalled one minute on air. You couldn't get better than that. I would raise the parking boom at quarter to ten and at quarter to eleven I'd be off with guests and crew for a nightcap. I vaguely surmised that FtF's successor might be a little less leisure-friendly. I was right about the 'less' but way out with regard to the 'little'.

We missed the 'next week', of course, and the one after as well. Ten pm on Tuesday was filled with fillers, 'Penguins of Antarctica' sort of stuff, staples. Meanwhile I adjusted tardily to the time-frames of canned TV.

The Face the Fax era had meant a few phone calls and a bit of moonlighting. To start with I persuaded myself that this new era would mean an accelerated version of the same, and I hung on to my various existing jobs. Principally this meant The Star, where I was theoretically one of the thundering herd of assistant editors. In addition there was 702, which was Monday nights plus its own bit of phoning, conferring, and lining-up.

Then there was our minuscule clothing company, Seffricana Pridewear, a two-man operation by which I and my wife Gael produced a variety of ties on the theme of the South African flag. I had two five-minute TV slots a week — a newspaper review in the early morning and an entrepreneurship interview on a programme called Your Own Business (known to aficionados as 'yob'). I had two small-time corporate consultancy-type jobs, each mainly entailing a single monthly meeting. I was doing bits and bobs of the speechifying circuit, a ludicrously lucrative pursuit which was usually too alluring to refuse (and because I couldn't refuse some of the paid engagements I found it also impossible to refuse some of the unpaid ones — churches and schools and Rotaries — for fear of turning myself into a mercenary). Various foreign freelance writing assignments were compelling, for the similarly sordid reason that they paid in sterling and deutschmarks that converted well into the ravaged rand, and March '95 was seeing the second edition of Sidelines.

This was a satisfactory range of pursuits, not to say crowded, and sensibly viewed there was no room for another, but I tried it anyway and immediately began to feel the heavy smite of overload.

Initially it wasn't so much time on the clock as space in the head. All these new decisions! Like who was to be my new partner.

On the Fax I had been a part-time employee of the SABC, simple. Now I was a contractor to the SABC, whole new ballgame. I was all of a sudden in the big league, and it took a while for the penny to drop.

That makes more sense if you know that I came to it as a guy with a long and ingrained history of sukkeling. I had spent most of my adult life in a brand of genteel poverty, preoccupied with fighting the great anti-apartheid fight according to my own idiosyncratic lights. In particular I had spent more than a decade, from my 33rd year to my 45th, going systematically broke as owner, editor, and bottle-washer of Frontline magazine, which had been all very high-minded and award-winning and so forth but was perpetually on the bones of its financial posterior. Although the graph had turned well upward in the last while I had been so long and so far from the big-time stakes that I took it for granted that a venture like this was bound to be another penny-pinching exercise, and I would have to cajole and wheedle some production company to co-operate.

At first I assumed I would necessarily be the sub-contractor: that some middle-size production house would sign up with the large-size SABC, and sub-sign with small-size me. That seemed logical and natural, and it was a profound shock to discover that the giant corporation was perfectly willing to contract with me and leave me to distribute the enormous sums involved in shooting, editing and packaging a 45-minute documentary. This discovery was vouchsafed in a cartoon-style encounter with one of the corporation's financial managers. He was going up an up escalator and I was going down the down one. While the fingers of fate pulled us apart, voices raising like a volume knob being turned up and faces and figures and shopping-bags floating silently into sightline, he changed my life.

'So where's your contract?'

'I don't know who to do it through.'

'No, man, do it direeeeeeeect.'

His last word echoed through the ether as his visage disappeared into the throng. It was a revelation. Not that there has been a divorce in the ensuing relationship or even any stormclouds, but that if ever a stormcloud might arise it is a good deal better to be the party in the driving seat.

Who, however, was to be the subcontractor? I had two sets of friends in the business, both well up at the top of the tree. Richard Beynon and Marie Bruyns ran Facet Films. I had done odd jobs for them, aside from having been a friend of Richard's since Noah was a baby. Roberta Durrant and her husband Uwe Jantsch were Penguin, a company which had more of the characteristics of the eagle as author of a whole series of high-flying productions ranging from Future Imperfect to Going Up.

Knowing a sum total of nought about the applied economics of television, I had only the dimmest of notions, even after the escalator encounter, of how desirable a property I was sitting on. I did, however, feel vastly complected about having to choose either Facet or Penguin over the other. When an SABC heavyweight pointedly remarked that 'Penguin have plenty of work here, things must be shared,' I took that as more than a hint and contacted Facet. I was still uneasy nonetheless and the unease sharpened when the discussion with Marie and Richard went all wrong, taking me into Steps C, D, E, and subsequent — what equipment we'd be using when and where and how many day and night-time hours respectively we'd be allocating to on- and off-line editing respectively — while what I needed was the raw simple basic basics, Step A: how does this deal *work*?

That evening I played klaberjas with Patrick Lee and told him of these discomforts. It happened that I was feeling guilty about Patrick, because I was chairman of the judging panel of the Mondi Magazine Awards, which had recently administered to Patrick an honour which he considered very backhanded indeed.

He had done an imposing state-of-the-nation take-out in Style magazine, and he, and Style's editor Marilyn Hattingh, and Style's publishers Noel Coburn and Terry Moolman, and various other luminaries of the trade, and the punters at large, were betting on Patrick as shoo-in certainty to win the Features award.

This article had been one of those enviably talked-about ones since even before it was published. The buzz started spreading as soon as he sent a draft around for the once-over, even while it was getting its T's crossed and I's dotted, not to mention P's and Q's polished: 'Lee back in action; brilliant piece coming up in Style.'

So when the finalists were published with Patrick's name among them, that was no surprise. And since the other two finalists in this category both involved substantially humbler works in the women's magazine genre, one by Michelle Magwood and the other by Nomavenda Mathiane... well, if Patrick had been a horse his odds would have shrunk to about 1:10.

And so came the night, black tie and string quartet and specially designed chocolate logos on the dessert plate, the print media's glitterati gathered together by the thousand, and after due time and due suspense along rolled the Features category, tantantara.

By unhesitant convention, Features was the main thing. It carried the same prize money as all the rest, Health and Leisure and Design etc, but then, at the Artes awards Best Original Lighting Technique is nominally of the same stature as Best Actor. At the Mondi awards, Features is the equivalent of Best Actor and there were Patrick and Nomavenda and Michelle up on stage with their hearts in their mouths, and my heart was in my boots because I knew what was coming.

Which was that Patrick was called up first, to receive what I knew he was going to see (and did he just!) as the booby prize. Then came Noma-V which left Michelle as winner, to the surprise of all concerned and the chagrin of the Style contingent, various members of which have been making caustic cracks from that day to this.

I've been accused of everything from affirmative actionism to nepotism to gender paternalism to being threatened by Patrick's prowess. In fact I played no part in that decision other than keeping the debate — the most heated the judges ever had — to a semblance of procedural order. I firmly eschewed the expression of any view whatever, on the grounds that I was hopelessly compromised. Patrick was a very close buddy, Noma-V had not only been for many previous years my closest colleague but was also the godmother of my daughter Meave, Michelle's winning story quoted me, and the near-miss entries included another two by close friends and two more which had been shown to me as drafts and amended on my advice. Choosing the Features winners, I was out of.

Nonetheless I could feel how Patrick was feeling, tail end Charlie up on the stage. (The next year we changed the system precisely so as not to leave the third best of maybe a hundred entrants looking like a loser.) I felt guilty towards him. It was not that I couldn't see the logic of the decision. Grand in scale and slick in execution Patrick's story may have been, but it was over-written. It was too much. It felt like an essay out of Time magazine, full of In words and In references that you had to be an In person to make out.

That was what the judges' debate had been about, assessing Patrick's pyrotechnics against the heartfelt straightforwardness that both Michelle and Nomavenda had produced.

Whether the decision was right or not, who knows. It's not a marathon or a sprint or the 50 metres freestyle, where eyesight can give you an absolute ranking and electronics can refine it to the microsecond. Literary awards compare apples not only with oranges but with artichokes and turnips and garden benches and steel ceilings. Even when you did have two apples in a row, or two stories approximately equivalent in scope or scheme or subject, comparison was inevitably subjective to the point of whimsy.

Yes indeed, the judges had all sorts of scales and graphs and aids and guides, but putting words in order is not like putting bricks in order. How do you objectively measure Writer A, who gives you consistently solid workmanlike information, against

Writer B, who is slapdash and sloppy and sometimes loses you entirely but you keep on reading because at erratic intervals you find a phrase of genius, a comment or observation that makes you laugh or cry or think or remember, or all of the above?

Impossible. A year later, when Patrick was emigrating to England and I was emotional with the conflict between sorrow at friends' departure and anger at having their backs turned upon we who stay, I plucked up courage to tell him about the over-writing thing and to defend the decision as an honest one. That was a load off the mind, but until then I had a constant discomfort at the back of the mind; a bad image of Patrick and his wife Sandi and the entire regiment of magazine mafiosi disbelieving their ears when he was pipped to the post by a couple of outsiders.

So while — between klaberjas hands and long before I had unloaded the mind — I was regaling Patrick with the bafflement of this unwont choice, my subconscious was acutely conscious of a sense of owing him one. Patrick listened to my worries about favouritism and finally came up with the Solomonianly obvious thing: 'So don't take anyone you know, take someone you don't, and it so happens that my friend Keith Shaw is in any case the quintessential man for the job.'

Technically I did know Keith, but only on How-are-you-Fine-thanks terms that didn't count. I rang Keith and we arranged to meet at a coffee bar, 10 am Saturday.

Friday afternoon a fax from an old friend, Simon Nash, told me that the forces of evil (I paraphrase, but only slightly) were on the point of demolishing the old Rosebank post office, and good men and true would gather to fight the good fight at 10 am on the morrow.

I phoned Keith again with Plan B. Instead of slurping the processed bean while we talked turkey, we would do a prototype right then and there. Would he kindly arm himself with a camera, and we'd take the Rosebank post office as the peg for programme one: urban conservation.

Keith was bok, if somewhat bemused, and ten o'clock found us shaking hands at the corner of Oxford and Baker, while Simon Nash rallied the faithful with song and dance a loudspeaker's distance up the road.

So far so good. We were both present and correct and the sun was shining. But the rest was downhill. Keith couldn't believe that I wanted to just walk up to the post office and go. Where was script? Where was schedule? Where was plan? Then, when we'd established that walk up and go was to be the programme's essence and script and all, we discovered that the sound system was blown.

For twenty minutes we fiddled with equipment. At any rate Keith fiddled with equipment, feeling unmistakably skaam about scrabbling about with screwdriver on the flagstones of a public pavement in the heartland of his Old Boys Club. I looked on with what was supposed to pass as an expression of intelligent interest but in fact was a combination of blank ignorance, vis-à-vis the technical hitch, acute frustration, vis-à-vis the protest winding towards a tantalising end in the distance, and solidifying doubt, vis-à-vis Keith.

Finally Keith diagnosed a dud microphone cable and said we needed a replacement from his office 'just along the road in Corlett Drive'. True enough one end of Corlett Drive is 'just along the road' but the other is a couple of busy kilometres beyond that. With a mental picture of my first programme vanishing before the mind's eye I retrieved my combi and off we went.

When we got back the protest was still, unexpectedly, on the go and, an hour late, we did indeed walk up and go. I was lugging a cable-borne microphone with, as I later realised, a total lack of awareness that the cameraman might be anything less than an omnipotent and omnisighted creature who ought instantly to see and focus on anything that happened to be in my mind. Keith was being plunged back into cameraman days, a period several years earlier in his career, and was not

17

surprisingly perceiving matters the way that cameramen should perceive matters.

Cameramen, for instance, would automatically distinguish the interview from the setting-up. You weren't meant to be rolling while your client, or presenter, or whoever, was saying 'hullo, we're doing a TV programme' or 'would you mind if we came in and looked around' and the like. They started rolling when you'd sorted that stuff out; when your guest had straightened his cuffs and checked his cowslick and turned his best side to camera and put on his public-performance smile. *That* was when you switched on.

Which was sensible enough, but was not what I wanted. When we knocked at the post office gates for an in situ assessment we were met by two extremely large gentlemen with gel in their hair and regulations in their hearts. Regulations said, evidently, that the public was verbode in post office premises other than on the right side of the counter during working hours. The large gentlemen explained this in delicious detail while I was frantically signalling behind my back that Keith should kindly record this exchange. Keith, waiting for us to get inside so we could start work, was impatient with these obstructive characters getting in the way and mystified by my sudden succumbment to an apparent epileptic attack.

Moreover, Keith took it for granted that our business would be to grasp the holy cause and propagate it. So did Simon Nash and the various actors and showbiz ouens and other arties who were gracing the ranks of the protesters. (Indeed, who virtually *were* the ranks of the protesters, aside from a hired band.)

The holy cause, jackpot first time, was the cause of opposing the wicked money-grubbing developers who were intent on wrecking our heritage for the sake of lucre. What everybody expected of the media, and had expected even before the onset of the New SA and the constitutionalising of political correctness, was to serve the side of the angels. (And nobody expected it more than the boss of the development company, who was a few days later dragged kicking and screaming to the site, convinced that our purpose was to invest him with horns and a long red tail.)

But even if I didn't know anything that mattered about this programme — what it was to be called, who was to produce it, what demographic audience it was aimed at, anything — I did know one thing, so firmly entrenched in the back of my mind that I had perhaps failed to articulate it. This was that it was not going to automatically take the obvious lines.

My private definition of objectivity had always been that you look for the good in the side you don't like and the faults in the side you do. I am as keen as the next man, which actually means a heck of a lot keener than 99% of next men, to pursue grace and elegance in city and in nation. But I was not about to anoint Simon Nash with a halo; still less to paint the developer as a cardboard villain. I wanted to explore the *other side* that there always is, which in this case would mean a few aback-taking questions for Simon. Also a bit of unwelcome querying of the received verities such as that that that is old is identical with that that is sacred and that that that is erected is necessarily poorer than that that is demolished.

Keith was as aback-taken by this unexpected approach as Simon, and deeply doubtful that, whyever it was that I was doing whatever it was that I was doing, the SABC was going to swallow a jot of it. Communication can not be said to have been telepathic.

Then again, what was one to expect of a prototype? By the end of the morning we had on tape a kind of weird something.

I said: 'If you'll process your film I'll think around what else we need.'

Keith gave me a long look that wondered why this escaped journo didn't get harmlessly back behind a typewriter, and said: 'Process? This is videotape. There's no processing.'

Keith went home and I bet poured himself a stiff one and told his wife that he'd wound up with superdumbo.

I went home and poured myself a quart and told my wife I had to look further. Which I did, for a few desultory days, but Keith had had a certain twinkle in the corner of the eye and what is more he had trod the sidewalk and toted the camera, while everyone else was talking figures over coffee cups, and Father Time was scything ever on. I went back to Keith and said 'let's do it', and he gulped a powerful gulp and said 'okay' and he called his chief lieutenant Donovan Marsh and, I later learned, said 'we've got into one strange thing here, so cross your fingers and pray'.

I'd got my job by accident. Now Keith had got his in much the same way. If there's one lesson that life delivers more consistently than all the rest, it's that the world works better by accident than design.

The Keith accident turned out to be a fine accident. He was and is the perfect partner and the company he runs fits the bill to a T. Over the duration of the Trek all of its people have been involved one way or another – often more than one way. Andrew Grealey, for one, has been cameraman, soundman, editor and director. Donovan, much the same. Keith has often himself led the editing through the incredibly detailed process of making a final cut out of source tapes. I've learned not only new respect for editors' skills but gratitude for their patience. I have learned, too, that the activity of editing for screen is so massively different from the activity of editing for the printer that it is misleading to call them by the same name. Among the editors who made sense out of the Trek are Brad Stillwell, Patrick Reilly, Patrick Lee and Dante Laudati. We've had several valued cameramen and numerous associates. For organisation we owe a lot to Michael Modena, Thami Moore and Hubert Khumalo. Plenty of others have been involved, in plenty of other ways. However, in terms of the kilometre-covering Trekking per se there are three people above all who have made the thing work: Richard Burnett, Louis Ndlovu and Joe Dlamini, much appreciated Trekkers.

3

Disengaging

So a partnership was in place. What wasn't in place was a name, and you can't have a programme without a name. It was fine for Shakespeare and Juliet to wax philosophical about the smell of roses and the vacuity of names, but they didn't live in the TV era. Nature abhors an incomplete schedule, and the SABC is a child of nature. There was a big empty spot from 10 to 10.45 Tuesday nights, former slot of Face the Fax and now a glaring lacuna. They needed words to write on the timetable; they needed words to send the newspapers. And I couldn't think of the words.

We went through a multitude. Keith punted What's Bothering Beckett? I was bothered by the 'bother', and also didn't want my name in the title; seemed arrogant and cocky. I wanted 'Seffrica', a word I revel in as the phonetic rendering of the way the average South African pronounces the place he belongs to. Everybody else said Seffrica was confusing and low-rent. It makes you say 'huh?' said someone; someone else

wondered who'd want to watch a programme that sounded like Gammattaal.

Keith was strong on the need for my name, which he saw as a licence to hold opinions, especially opinions which might embarrass the Corp. We tried compromises: It's My Country; My Kind of Country; the 'my' being a substitute licence. Unfortunately every possible permutation of 'country' conjured up images of drawling southern Americans in stetsons, and the alternative, 'nation', came across as stilted and pompous in any combination we could think of.

Patrick Lee came up with Skew View, Subjective Onlooker, the rather delicious Crap Detector, and dozens more. We tried Afrikaans names, and turned them down as sectional, not to say suicidal. We tried Zulu names, and turned them down as corny. Everybody and his uncle was slamming bits of token Zulu onto every product and promotion you could think of, trying to shloep the new establishment.

I latched on to Native Land, despite objections that 'native' was still ambiguous in the SA context, but by this time Keith was pushing for a Seffrican amendment, A Sip of S'effrika. I bought that one for a while, in writing even, but then underwent a midnight mind-change and woke up in shivers about the flimsiness of 'sip'.

NNTV's congenial promotions lady, Margaret Ndlokwana, was on the point of having kittens. It was about to be a case of pin the tail on the donkey when out of the blue appeared a fax from Gus Silber with a whole flotilla of names mainly based around the terms 'safari' and 'trek'. Seffrican Safari cropped up, Seffrica displaying an admirably obstinate unwillingness to lay down and die. So did Off the Beaten Trek, and Beckett On Trek.

Patrick was heatedly anti Trek, arguing that while it might display a certain alluring assonance of the short 'e' when combined with Beckett, beyond that it had all the wrong connotations. For me, though, trek is one of those few of our home-grown words that has truly permeated the English

22

language, and its connotations were a long way up on 'safari', which conveys upper-class ladies with painted fingernails buying designer pith helmets for a weekend at a game lodge.

Eventually it was one of those last-minuters. Margaret was on the phone for the 257th painstaking time, speaking slowly as to a little child, asking whether I had yet made up my tiny mind. 'Beckett's Trek', I blurted forth, and there it was, and it was a blurt I never regretted.

I've taken two seriously unregrettable steps in my time. One was committing matrimony in 1973 and the other was, at much the same time, abandoning a legal career in favour of the wilds of journalism.

Journalism might lack status, income, and security, and the proverbial Jewish mama never shot her mouth off with pride about her daughter marrying a journalist. In fact she probably changes the subject. But that's because she, like most of mankind, is deaf to the two incredibly fundamental benefits of the trade.

One is that it is inherently interesting. You can make it boring, of course, like you can make anything boring, but you have to work at it. Not infrequently, in the more statusful and opulent professions it's the other way round.

Whatever the journos' problems, whatever the public images of scavengers shoving flash bulbs up the noses of murderers and politicians, I've never been sorry to be in it. A job with a built-in interest factor is a rarer privilege than is generally recognised.

But the interest factor is small stuff compared to the other privilege, the ability to make up your own mind. As a lawyer, or for that matter a corporate exec or a politician or a PR consultant, you take the line you have to take. You take your client's line, or the corporation's line, or the party's line. As a journalist, or in any case my kind of journalist, you take your conscience's line. That must be the eighth wonder.

The little chance decision about a name for a TV programme was hardly in the same league, but irrational as may be it ranks in my head as part three of a trilogy of correct choices. Even before the name settled in and became a noticeable koppie on the electronic landscape, I felt confident that we had touched each necessary base: the licence element, the indigenous element, the questing element. As for the arrogance and cockiness of shoving my own personal handle onto the logo, that had already become secondary to the far vaster arrogance of assuming a right to shout the odds in a million living rooms every week.

But no sooner had Margaret got off my back with a name than her colleague Hannatjie Fourie was on it for a programme. And this was a problem. For one thing, at Keith's initiation we had developed cold feet in respect of the post office and urban conservation, on the good grounds that this stuff was too easy. We were meant to be exploring South Africa, its breadth its depth its diversity. How could we start with a first, formative, scene-setting episode based in dear sweet Rosebank, not only the national capital of yuppiedom but also the site of the very Woolworths which put the cornflakes on both his breakfast table and mine? Too close, too cosy, too cliquey.

Then there was another small thing. Keith was developing a theme song, one that he has since refined to a mantra. It goes, through clenched teeth in the artificially dulcet tones that you adopt to disguise the urge to kill:

'Denis, this is full time work.'

In theory I already had full-time work, in the service of that august journal The Star. Whilst the term 'full-time' in this context should not be read excessively literally (and we were soon to formalise a half-pay arrangement), I was peculiarly loath to chuck up the newspaper connection.

To Keith, this was an irrationality of asylum proportions. To other friends too, particularly given that I made no secret, inside the building or out, of my view that the paper was terminally dreary.

My employers at the paper had a different view; namely, that readership surveys kept telling us the public thought we were the best thing since candy floss. This view raised questionmarks in the minds of we the unenlightened, as the same public was also avidly honing the ability to keep its hand in its pocket when the newsvendors came by. But management explained that declining circulation proved the success of the grand plan to consolidate our reach in the most commercially viable quarters, and when that left heads being scratched the managers brandished the balance sheet, which indeed miraculously seemed to demonstrate that the lower the circulation the greater the profit.

My variance from approved opinion on the care and conduct of the paper was by no means career-enhancing. Twenty years previously I had been a crown prince at the same institution to which, returned with greying hair and amplified waistline, I now fitted the role of court jester or 'loose cannon' (that phrase got used so often it was like a job title). It was a perverse progression but had its rewards, and the establishment seemed to feel it was nice to have some cussed bugger around to make everybody feel righteous for permitting dissent. I was kept well away from authority, mind, lest I publish something that might cause pursed lips. So my so-called 'editorial' role amounted to two simple functions. I wrote a twice-a-week column, which I wanted and the establishment tolerated, and I attended the daily 10 am leader conference, which I tolerated and they wanted.

At leader conference we batted out the paper's view on the mighty issues of the day, and often as not I ended up wordsmithing the emergent view. My alleged value to this process was firstly to argue the toss at conference, which had tended to become a ten-second rubber-stamp delivering the obvious verdict on anything from the Middle East to street urchins, and secondly to write the stuff in a way that attempted to keep the reader awake.

Somewhere my footsteps had strayed drastically from the fast track, but it was not an especially worrisome straying. Whatever I thought of The Star as a piece of reading or as an organisational entity, as a human environment it was fine, and still is. I enjoy the interactions there, in corridors and canteen as much as conference room.

So that was one reason for not quitting. Another was that I had little faith in the prognosis for the Trek. One day I'd get home and there'd be a terse message on the answering machine. I wanted a port of call reasonably near to hand rather than have to tramp the streets with a c.v. and a wan job-seeking smile.

Another was that I'd worked for this company six times, starting as a 16-year-old schoolkid. I'd walked out once and been fired once (made the scapegoat for the banning of The World). I'd kept on coming back — this last time as a result of an act of great nobility by the then bosses, Jolyon Nuttall and Richard Steyn, in buying over my bankrupt magazine Frontline a short step before the tattooed guys came around with iron bars.

I won't say it was pure nobility, as it also provided The Star with a handy assessed tax loss and with the services of two sets of hands — mine and Nomavenda's — that at the time it thought it wanted, but fundamentally I owed a great deal to Jolyon and Richard. Oddly, I was still sitting in my actionably airless cubbyhole, laughingly termed an 'office', long after both of them had been manoeuvred out in that metal-hearted manner that corporations have.

At least they outlasted Noma-V, whose particular brand of brilliance fitted nowhere in The Star's lexicon. Some of the stuff that Noma-V had done for me was weirdly wonderful, giving non-Sowetans in general and whiteys in particular a truly unparalleled taste of the kind of township talk and feelings that could sometimes knock your eyes out. Two compilations of her

Frontline writing have been published as books — one in America, where else?, followed by one at home — but she and The Star didn't belong together.

Once she wrote a riveting account of Mandela (well before his presidency and canonisation) facing down the Black Lawyers' Association, a bunch of Africanists who had beforehand widely advertised to all and sundry that they were going to give the old sellout what-for. Now Mandela was waiting for the what-for, and he was saying so loudly and repeatedly and with the kind of rank stubbornness that few people on this planet can get away with, while the Africanists hummed and hawed and studied their shoes and hoped frantically that someone would stand up and speak.

Noma-V described it in knuckle-curlingly glorious (albeit as usual sloppy and misspelt and ungrammatical) detail. The Star didn't publish it. Noma-V spoke to me and I spoke to the relevant editor, who after a long vent of indignation on the subject of the slop and the spelling and the grammar (the panel-beating of which is to my mind an occupational hazard of editing in SA) finally said: 'And anyway it's not a story; nothing happens.'

They probably filled the space with an analysis of the Two Chinas policy. Or maybe a pseudo-psycho dissection of an alleged 'trend' about to overwhelm California. We were good at those.

The cock-ups at The Star were truly heroic. Sometimes you'd expect to find them in jokebooks or satires, and some deserve their tiny place in history, such as the time the Deputy Ed, Rex Gibson, persuaded me to write a piece about a survey on the parties' political support. At this stage I was 45 years old and was supposedly some sort of asteroid in the journalistic firmament, and this was the kind of job usually done by a junior reporter between lunchtime and sundowner.

However Rex's case was logical and indeed derived from my own oft-repeated insistence that our business was meant to be the business of making the written word a joy to read. I had argued that we couldn't sommer give people in the morning the same information that had been on the radio news yesterday at 1 pm and 2 pm and 3 pm and 4 pm, and on the box at 6 pm and and 9 pm and at 7 am. It had washed through them all those times anyway, when they were imbibing it through that most user-friendly of organs, the ear. Now we expected them to apply the rigorous discipline of the eye to reading the same stuff, usually put together as if designed by a Goldfinger commissioned by the electronic media to kill off the press.

Political support surveys were washouts for the newspapers, as the juicy bits were lightly gutted in the radio bulletins and the public cared not a whit for the refinements. So, said Rex, here was a day to put sermon to practice.

Okay. It was a challenge. Give it a go. I just had one little problem, which was the mangling that invariably took place at the hands of the sub-editors.

The subs were used to receiving copy that was too long for the space they had to put it in. They were also used to copy that left gaps and questions and non-sequiturs, and to panel-beating it ferociously. My practice was to do the stuff in exactly the way I expected to see it published, down to the last comma. With the subs who subbed my column, I had a perfect relationship. The column was 50 cms. I would do it to 50 cms. They would normally put it through unaltered. Where they did want to alter it, they would give me a ring and say, in varied degrees of politeness or forthrightness according to personality, where they thought I'd screwed up. We'd discuss it, we'd agree, and bob's yr uncle. Where I wasn't in reach and there was a problem, they'd apply discretion, and because of the satisfactory basic relationship the discretion was almost always satisfactory discretion. Of the hundreds of columns I've written for The Star, the number that led to writer-sub conflicts can be counted on my thumbs.

Unconventionally and paradoxically, this procedure led to the subs arguing about my copy *more* than they argued with anybody else.

In general on receipt of copy from news reporters they would groan the ritual groan, mutter the ritual mutter about declining standards and where did these people go to school, roll up their sleeves and slash the hatchet until they had a brand of order.

The copy they got from the panoply of Eds — Asst Eds and Dep Eds and Eds-in-Chief and whathaveyou — they would groan about less frequently albeit sometimes more deeply, and employ a diplomatic scalpel or, at most, rapier in preference to the hatchet. Mostly, though, they would not even think of discussing the Eds' copy with the Eds at all, let alone challenging the Eds in terms of 'this point could be better made' or 'the middle bit here is floppy and confusing' or 'damn sombre, couldn't we have a joke or two on the way'.

The column relationship I had with the subs is the way the writer-sub relationship ought to work, and one of the reasons the print media are in the dwang is that it is so rare. (Of course my own little publications, where I vigorously practise the editorial side of the same relationship, are endemically in worse dwang than anyone else in print, but that is for different reasons.)

My copy, they'd readily argue about anything from the overall message to the stylistic flaws of paragraph eleven to where I could use non-English expressions without the obligatory italics (it being a deliberate habit of mine to incorporate bits of indigenous languages into a Seffrican English). They did it because I embraced it and actively asked for it. Sometimes I'd agree, and as a rule it was my fingers on my keyboard that made the changes. Sometimes I'd privately disagree but make a change anyway, in appreciation. Sometimes, of course, no change, but even then the listening and discussing would have done wonders to deflect the subs instinct as reflected on a poster I kept on my office wall:

The strongest drive is not Love or Hate, it is one person's need to change another's copy.

amend / revise / alter / chop to pieces / modify / change

Unfortunately the column relationship was seldom carried over to other articles, where the sub with X amount of space would inevitably have X + Y amount of copy to fit into it. For this reason I had by this time already flatly stopped writing anything but my column, and for this reason Rex's challenge gave me a dose of collywobbles.

'Rex,' I said, 'how much?'

'Make it 45 centimetres,' he said.

I said: 'Rex, if I write 45 cms will you make sure that the whole 45 cms appears intact?'

'Of course,' said Rex in the airy way favoured by very senior mahogany editors when they talk of their influence over the conduct of lowly coalface editors. 'I'll see to it.'

It was a Friday and I worked most of the weekend at the task of making survey figures sing. By Sunday night, they sang. I had a piece I was quietly content to hand in. I awaited with more glee than I like to admit Rex's grudging congratulations to come.

On Monday morning I swanned cheerfully into the coalface, virtuous as can be, and deposited not 44,9 cms, not 45,1 cms, but 45 cms right on the nose into the awaiting electronic desk. To improve the shining hour I even popped my head past the door of the page editor, a curmudgeonly character who had once been a big-shot somewhere and was now resentfully working out the hours until he qualified for a pension. (He quit on the very day, I believe.)

He looked at me and said: 'It's five past nine.'

I looked at my watch and affably seconded this assertion. 'Yes,' I said, 'it is indeed five past nine.'

'Deadline,' he said, 'is 9 o'clock. I need time to edit this stuff.'

Alarm bells rang, but I let it be. The day was bespoken by another activity. Any case, once he'd read it he'd be happy. I crossed fingers and hoped for the best, unconvincingly telling myself that I was too old and ugly to worry.

But the piece would have my name on it, and one does get jumpy about taking the public rap for someone else's anonymous incompetence. So come Tuesday I took up the paper with a certain anxiety . . . and it was worse than the worst possibility.

Among other things, the 45 cms had shrunk to 38. There were jokes that had lost their punchlines. There were intact references to excised sentences. There was one place where some wholly gratuitous monkeying had made me an insane liar. The list of damage was long and painful.

Also, there was a strange thing. The story had involved a million percentages, which I typed as '%'. The published version had them all changed to 'percent', which, I worked out, had added 7 cms to the length, so that in real terms my 45 cms had shrunk to not 38 but 31.

I enquired. The page editor said 'style book'. Indeed the style book specified 'percent' and not '%'. I wondered why, and the page editor said why did it matter why? The style book had spoken, and that was enough for him.

It intrigued me. Given the constant quest to include as much text as design considerations permit, why insist on a 7-character word when conventional usage takes a 1-character synonym for granted?

I went to ask the guy who wrote the style book. He stared at the relevant entry for a very long time as if hoping that an explanatory apparition would appear on the page, and finally said: 'You know, that's a good question.'

I tried editors, I tried old hands. Finally I met a guy from the works, who said, no, simple, there'd been some trouble with a batch of low-grade flong in about 1965 and the intricate % had risked coming out as a blur, so the 'percent' had been a precaution.

Flong was a cardboardy part of a production process that went obsolete more than twenty years ago.

I was reminded of a terrific tale in the autobiography of Stafford Cripps, who was Brit ambassador to Moscow in World War II.

One day Cripps is walking with Stalin in the grounds of the Winter Palace. They come upon a sentry on duty in the middle of nowhere. Cripps says: 'What's he doing here?' Stalin asks the sentry 'What are you doing here?' The sentry says 'Corporal told me to stand here.' Stalin calls the corporal who says the sergeant told him to have someone there; the sergeant says the lieutenant told him; the lieutenant says the captain; and so on, up to the general. Stalin invokes the army historians, who discover that one morning in 1768 Catherine the Great found an early spring flower at that spot. 'Ooh, commander,' she said, 'what a lovely flower. Make sure nobody stands on it.' And 175 years of round-the-clock protection ensued.

The Star's encrustations manifested in other ways too, the leaders being an example. The paper had a long history of vacuous and soporific leaders, and while my leaders were in theory appreciated as being vigorous and pointed etc, the appreciation was sometimes very double-edged. One exalted personage had a favourite phrase, 'going off pop', a thing he urged me not to do every time I was writing a leader. Going off pop could mean saying anything that anybody might take offence at or could mean saying anything at all in tones other than the time-honoured measured literary leader-voice.

32

Once I'd done a punchy leader, machine-gun style as opposed to regular leadery lecturiness, about township disorder, inter alia expressing disapproval of the failure of the black leadership to lead. This was too much for the establishment, and it got bowdlerised into a bland little well-pronounced item saying nothing.

Next day I retaliated, somewhat underhand, by making a list of leader clichés — 'cool heads are needed', 'decisive action must be taken', 'let reason prevail', 'thorough enquiry is necessary', etc — and seeing if I could cram them all into one leader. I did. It went down fine. To this day the library contains one particular leader with every known leader cliché. You could look it up, except you'd have difficulty being sure which it was.

I shouldn't yap at the hand that sort-of feeds me — I'm still an associate ed at The Star, where these comments may not go down big — but I have a fondness for the place no matter what and I find it upsetting to see it steadily slide downhill from its long and noble tradition of mediocrity. Perhaps there is value in somebody saying in public what everybody says around the tea urn: the paper feels moribund. It needs a wake-up call.

I was building up to confessing the other reason why, despite Keith's urgings, I wouldn't quit. It is because The Star is in town, and I increasingly valued the town connection.

This of course is nowadays a taste so rare as to not merely raise eyebrows but send them into tailspins. Middle-class whiteys are supposed to abhor and fear town, advance base of the encroaching third world. I think town is pretty nice, overall. It would be nicer for a somewhat less pungent scent of urine in the alleys, also for a revision of the general African worldview that God designed beer bottles, polystyrene, and chips packets to be the lilies of the urban field, but even as it is it is darem orraait.

Town has life and vibe and hawkers, who are one of the more admirable breeds of humankind along with nurses and volunteer firemen. Hawkers aren't necessarily in it for reasons of innate nobility, but heck, they add! I had a fifty-metre walk from garage to office, a walk past ten hawkers, and they were a daily uplift. How these guys kept body and soul together, with their humble cardboard trays of boiled sweets and roasted peanuts, heaven knows, but they were a perpetually smiling, amiable, trustworthy bunch. Right across town, the same description held weight. They'd feed your parking meter; they'd check that you'd picked a good apple; they'd give you a greeting to light your day. I could never understand the pinstripe set muttering and mumbling about how the pavements were a disgrace; as far as I could see the pavements were fundamentally a pride.

Maybe in some deep corner I enjoyed the rare status of being a white man on foot in town. In my time I had seen the city centre Library Gardens, for example, move from a 99% white population through the whole spectrum to the opposite, and the funny thing was that the rare whitey still there would feel an unmistakably good vibe from the blacks around; a kind of silent 'thankyou for not turning your back on us'. But in a bigger corner I regretted the defection of the bourgeoisie.

Running became the order of the day. In the drawing rooms of elegance it used to be said 'you don't go south of the railway line'. That became 'you don't go south of Braamfontein', which turned to 'south of Empire road'. Currently the big thing is south of Loch avenue and the trendsetters are into south of Westcliff drive. They will soon have locked themselves into nowhere south of Broederstroom and they'll be running still.

I don't want to run from Africa, I want to embrace it, and town is a daily embrace. I don't want to be bitten by the Sandton Syndrome, proceeding in locked car from locked home to locked office and treating public places as a staging post to Hades. In my experience the terrors of the city increase in direct proportion to one's distance away from the city. Not to deny that the crime factor could be a bastard, to shop-owners especially, but that was true of the leafy north too.

Town, more than the other places, was doubly frightening to those who never saw it. They'd sit in Bryanston or Bordeaux and see the headlines – of the THREE KILLED IN TOWN TODAY brand – and freak. Partly that was because THREE MILLION HAVE PERFECTLY SATISFACTORY DAY IN TOWN is no headline. Being there, day by day, greeting the doorman, sampling the hawkers' nartjies, chatting to the kids at the walkaround chess set ... this stuff kept me sane, and more than that, cheerful. Sufferers from the spreading epidemic of Sandton Syndrome will say that the notions 'sane' and 'cheerful' constitute a contradiction in terms, and who am I to say they can't be right? All I know is that when I meet the Syndrome mob and say 'how's things?' they trip over their lips and drool out a half-hour dirge about what a pity we don't live in Toronto. If you ask the same question around town you'll get great face-splitting beams and confident assurances of 'fust cluss' and 'hunnerd pussent'.

It's not only from the darkies either. Of the whiteys who still walk around town – stockbrokers like David Cobbett, lawyers like George Bizos and Derek Reid – I would say many feel rather like I do. You feel connected, you feel you belong. I'll readily say I wouldn't want to live there, and I admit I'm not lightly about to walk across town after dark, but if you look at town with both eyes it shows some of the features to love about Africa as well as some of the other thing.

For me there are no two ways about the cheer that town creates. The sanity is more subjective, but then there has traditionally been a confusion about which side of the asylum door is the inside and which the out. Those who wish to call us crazy are welcome, but we town people notice that while we walk free with a spring in our step our critics huddle by with worried frowns. The Star, to its credit, continues to inhabit the city that made it, and being there gives me a regular antidote to the lurking virus of the Sandton Syndrome. For that reason above all, I wouldn't quit it.

35

4
Kick-Hof

Given the immediacy of the commission, it was awfully long before we got onto Episode 1. Partly, we needed the right programme to start on and couldn't work out what it was. (At the time I thought we would battle to sustain 13 programmes. Now I'd take on a thousand if I had the chance.) To compound the delay my diary was cluttered with appointments made BT, Before Trek, which moved Patrick to heights of caustic disapproval. He thumped tubs and yelled that this was the best darn TV prospect there ever had been and I was jeopardising it by serving out the large range of prior commitments which he collectively dismissed as 'taking tea at Sauer street'.

Finally two free days were upcoming, a Thursday and a Friday. This had to be it, but where was the 'it'? On the Wednesday afternoon, Keith was climbing walls. I said: 'Right. Bloemhof.'

Bloemhof is a dorpie in the far south west of what was the Transvaal, the bit the world forgets because we associate south with Vereeniging and west with Lichtenburg and ignore the long leg that pirhouetted diagonally down the river towards Kimberley.

For all but two brief moments in its lifetime Bloemhof has been inflicted with the fate of explaining to outsiders, 'No, Bloem*hof*, not *-fontein*'.

The first exception was in the 1890s, when Bloem*hof* blipped the stock exchange boards as the putative site of the new-and-improved Kimberley. The diamond trail brought a tidal wave of fortune hunters and spawned three daily English newspapers. The diamonds however failed to live up to the prospectus. The Engelse departed to the extent that of the 13 000 current residents a sum total of 1 knows the tongue of Her Britannic Majesty as his home language, and the town embarked upon a hundred years of placidity interrupted on the morning of Saturday May 22, 1993, when the Transvaal awoke to the yellow-and-black posters of the Saturday Star proclaiming

TVL TOWN
FIRES ALL
BLACK
WORKERS

which seemed drastic even by the standards of that tense and pre-bill-of-rights era. This was the employers' response to a protest stayaway called by the local ANC, and was a knockout story for a media world slavering for a good clean evils-of-apartheid thriller.

By nightfall the place was knee deep in flak jackets and video cameras, and by the following Tuesday it was the site of the long-awaited South African armageddon, with every newspaper at home and abroad copiously quoting AWB spokesmen in respect of their intentions to imminently decimate the black population. Some also found some suitably violent replying affidavits from the black side, on how the township was now

37

no go for whites, and Bloemhof saw more headlines in those four days than in the last century collectively.

Intending to write a backgrounder, I got there a couple of days later when it had slid off the boil for absence of bodies in the streets. I was always behind the times in these matters, which suited me fine as I had nil interest in the bodies and lots of interest in the whys, which invariably became more comprehensible as the adrenalin reduced. One discovery was that the 'AWB spokesmen' consisted mainly if not entirely of one Whitey van Eeden, a guy of extraordinary good looks and photogenic flamboyance but suffering from so loose a racial screw that the volk of Bloemhof tapped their heads when his name came up and couldn't understand why the media kept seeking him out. (The answer is: give your news editor a tongue-tied administrator in a brown suit saying 'we greatly respect our black people and are anxious for an early resolution' and alternative career paths will be mentioned. Give him a gun-heavy Nazi Adonis shrieking 'we're killing the kaffirs at midnight', and you get an honorary invite to the executive luncheon.)

I was intrigued to find that the Bloemhof race war was only about 2% as warlike as it had been painted, and even that 2% was largely accidental, having started because the ANC faction, led by the gentlest gentlemanly schoolmaster in shoe leather, one Andrew Hanks, was a lot less strong in written English than in the spoken brand.

The ANCs were aggrieved about a whole range of issues, of which I outline one for flavour.

All the years the town's golf course had been, no surprise, for whites. With the recent thaw an agreement had been made that the course be de-whitened and what is more that the forthcoming annual tournament would be specifically non-racial.

This, thought the township residents or at any rate the leadership echelon, was nice. Their golfers would be up there in the lists, and at the 19th hole afterwards, symbolising the dawn of the new era.

Came the tournament and lo, the only dark complexions to swing an iron were complexions made in India. The African role was as usual to carry the bags and feel with toes for lost balls at the water hole. Disillusion took place.

When I heard this tale, told with hurt and pain and numbing sincerity by people who had waited aeons to belong and had now been unbelonged again — cynically, harshly, at their moment of hope — I was livid. When I later met an organiser of the golf day I was ready to jump down his throat with boots on. But he too had a tale — about the committee agonising over the two township entries that they had received, both from players who on their own evidence would score double figures on every hole. The same entries from white players would be turned down flat. Should it be different with the blacks? Should the rules be stretched to accommodate the aforementioned new era? If so, would it be a good start to have the new era's entrants duff their way round in excruciating inferiority to everyone else?

The end message of the golf affair was, yet again, the message that little is simple in the business of merging the cultures of southern Africa. But that message took a while to be heard. The first message, the message the township received in April 1993, was 'these whites are screwing us again'.

Disillusion — wellfounded, illfounded, and inbetween — was simultaneously taking place on several other fronts, and Hanks & Co decided to formalise their worries in a memorandum to the town council.

When they talked to me later they called this document a 'petition'. Reading it, the word 'petition' did not impinge itself. 'Ultimatum' would have been closer, but to convey the full feel of the thing 'declaration of war' would be best. If it had been expressly designed to put the whites' backs up it could hardly have done the job better, but it was by no means designed for that purpose. It was designed to set out an agenda for an earnestly requested meeting, and when the ANC guys *talked* to this agenda, it was as peaceable as you can imagine. Just that they couldn't set it across that way in writing.

I suspect that the ANCs had meantime realised this, because they were extremely coy about showing me their formative document. They talked *about* it, all right, and about the lousy white response to it, but when I wanted to see it, oops, everybody seemed to have left their briefcase at home.

Of course they may have been in a more belligerent frame at the time they wrote it, but even if so the sheer fact of the written message created its own momentum of aggro. For one thing the Boere's formal reply was also more uptight than it either needed to be or was intended to be, thus antagonising the Abantu who when they received it had no inkling of how much they had antagonised the Boere. Partly, of course, the Boere weren't feeling so much like Boutros-Ghali diplomats at the time they replied, but partly it was that they, too, were not thick with Shakespeares in their midst.

This exchange was the first glimmering I had of a knowledge that has grown a long way since: beware the written word. That seems upside down, I know. People of my caste and clime are taught from daddy's knee that when you want to make a deal into a proper deal you put it in writing. But daddy's knee wasn't into the business of finding harmony between the Abantu and the Boere writing to one another in a language that belongs to neither.

My '93 recce into the life and times of Bloemhof had awakened a taste. Two years later, how were things? This time I was there with a crew and a camera, and that made things otherwise for a start.

After five minutes in Bloemhof I learnt Lesson 1 of the Law of TV, which is that nothing distorts journalism as much as having a half-a-million rand TV camera peeking over your shoulder.

The camera distorts in two ways. The up side is that it opens doors like magic. Although it's a prime article of faith in quarters such as the alleged intelligentsia to say they never watch TV, aren't interested in TV, and so on, when you actually confront people with the rolling eye you're a welcome guest. I got to feel sore about the contrast between the long slow looks you could get as a print journo with a ballpoint and a notebook, and the Prince Charles treatment that the camera causes.

The down side is: showbiz takes over. Hardly anybody tells you the same thing the same way with the camera upon him as he happily said two minutes earlier in normal human-being conversation. It's frustration writ large. We're walking along, two piles of flesh and blood, regular people, and the guy I'm with makes a short sharp super comment that puts everything in perspective, and he does it with a twinkle and he does it as natural as can be. I say 'great!' and I turn to the cameraman, which is about 70% likely to be Richard Burnett or 20% to be Andrew Grealey, and say 'can I hear that please', and with luck Richard or Andy, or whoever of the 10%, promptly swings camera to shoulder and says 'go!' Without luck we have ten minutes of laying bars and changing tape and checking battery and preparing mike, and I say to the guy 'won't you say exactly what you just said', and he says 'sure', and shuffs his shoulders and straightens his back and flounces his hair and angles his best side to the camera, and adjusts his zippy one-liner into three paragraphs of qualifying sub-clauses and explanatory riders and long words that sound impressive.

You seldom get a truth on camera, and when you do you can seldomer use it, because there's another law, Law 2, which is that in the moments where the content is right then if the visual is right the audio is not right and if the audio is right the visual is not right and if the audio is right and the visual is right then the content has gone all to pot.

As a TV viewer I had frequently felt that the live TV debate, imposing unedited specialist woffle upon an unsuspecting public, ought to rank as a minor crime against humanity. In the Face the Fax era, seeing the same process from the inside out, I adjusted this view. I dropped the 'minor'. Starting the Trek I assumed that this problem was now disposed of: we would edit out the dull bits and streamline the confusing bits and thence would come the perfect documentary.

Well yes, after a fashion. There is something in that, and that the Trek has a viewership about twentyfold bigger than the Fax shows it. But don't overrate it. The idea that the Turbocube — the magical digital video edit system — can turn the sow's ear to silk purse is a mistake of colossal proportions and I started to learn about these rightaway.

Bloemhof was fascinating beyond my hope or expectation. For one thing we brought in a whole arena that I hadn't touched upon the last time: the delwers.

Delwers, diamond diggers, are a breed who belonged in the same compartment of the mind as Wyatt Earp or Zeederberg Stagecoaches — exotic, exciting, and expired. The image of delwer is an image of a tough little battler looking like a Before version of Barney Barnato, sleeping on his claim with a six-gun in his hand and a diamond pouch in his underpants. It is also an image of something extremely bygone, like spats or monocles or hansom cabs.

Well, here were delwers, genuine pistol-packing chance-taking delwers, 1995 vintage, spending their days twirling alluvial stones around sieves more ancient than spats or monocles. In every way the delwers' set-up was fantastical, and not all these ways were nice. For one, the social relationship also came from a pre-spats era, with the witbaas doing 100% of the guiding and ordering and a large number of downtrodden flattened-out darkies scurrying about like plantation slaves under Simon Legree.

At one point, at lunchtime, I noticed a whole workforce huddled under the floor of a large high trailer, crouching with the grease and the axles. It was a horribly dehumanising sight.

They looked like sheep; they looked as low and as humble and as hopeless as could be. They were there of their own accord, yes, to spend their lunchtime half-hour out of the sun, but they upset me.

I was getting on fine with the delwer, who regaled me with long stories about the high and mounting values per hectare of his various farms, and I brought up the thought that given all this good fortune it might be nice to see the guys under the trailer getting a little more belt out of life.

It wasn't as if he was upset or affronted; just that I may as well have been speaking Martian. Why the hell should they get more out of life? They're mos the volkies.

In the end we didn't broadcast that exchange; it was long, it was confusing, and a piece of noisy machinery started up in the middle. If the same thing came up again now, I would find a way to get the pith of it in. But in that earliest phase we adhered in more ways than now to the normal rules of TV, and what is more I had not yet discovered the interesting principle (which was to become the bane of my colleagues' lives) that a total lack of video edit learning or experience was no hindrance to getting into the edit suite and shrieking like hell.

In Bloemhof I saw a good deal of the phenomenon of the blacks as invisibles. It was what the new nation was supposed to have taken us past. It gave me a cramp, and even then it struck me — it's much worse now — that in the ranks of sociological distortion this New South Africa was shaping up to be a world beater. The public debate had become all about whether it was okay to overpromote a middle class handful by only five steps beyond their level of competence or whether it was better to go to ten; while on the fields and the shopfloors of vast parts of the nation you still weren't beginning to distinguish between a human being and a two-legged beast of burden.

Aside from the echoes of the Big Question, the delwers' tales were magnificent from beginning to end. One fellow had recently been victim of a multi-million rand diamond heist perpetrated by a former operative of the Dept of Civilian Co-operation, the thug-nest which initiated most of the apartheid dirty tricks that have bubbled to the surface of the cesspit. There had been false trays and false diamonds. There had been secret meetings and secret back-ups. There had been a gunfight at a hotel courtyard. It was all far too exotic to be true; which was one reason we didn't broadcast it. The other reason was the desperate non-fluency of my informant; we would have taken ten confusing minutes of air time to get the basics across.

A small problem here is: it *was* true. The bones of it have been borne out by some much-unpublicised court hearings. I guess the media in general were as perplexed as I was by all this incredible wealth of drama, and they too ducked it. To find the court records you must plough the small print in local papers, and the most interesting angle will never feature in court.

Not, anyway, like the delwer told it to me while we tromped through the lunar landscape that the Transvaal vlaktes look like after a hundred years of delwing. He talked of how the sudden loss of four million rands in diamonds had affected family relationships — between father and sons, between father and mother, between mother and sons, between those brothers who thought it a dumb idea to start with and those brothers who claimed they'd been going to cut the others in on the profits, and then, when you're prepared to get really hairy, between the sons' wives, the sisters-in-law.

This story was riveting and poignant, and was told to me in a wonderful African setting under a wonderful African sky in a wonderful African accent; and it died a death by archive. I was learning the price of canned TV. One cost of being able to cut the boring bits out is that you end up with far more than you can ever possibly use and you cut out half the good bits too.

Moreover, the good bits are often complicated and not immediately clear, and for TV purposes complicated is the twin brother of disaster. I try on the Treks to convey an element of the wealth and breadth and Seffricanness that comes across to me, but the Bloemhof expedition left me wondering how much of an element I was ever going to convey, and as time has gone by I have resigned myself to the answer: 'minuscule'.

Aside from the delwers, Bloemhof produced a trader who happily assured me (off camera) that he made R10 000 a week exploiting the school feeding system. This, he proudly stated, was not to be confused with the R12 000 a week his normal township food business delivered. Needing — shame — to supplement these humble earnings, he charged desperate mamas R5 a basket to collect prickly pears from his farm, which they would then sell on the roadside. I asked how long they'd typically take to sell a basket. He shrugged: 'A day, maybe, maybe two.' I asked what they'd sell their R5 investment for. He shrugged: 'R8, maybe R10 if it's a lucky day, maybe R3 and cut their losses.'

Sometimes I regret that we never went through a real wild thundering bolshevik up-against-the-wall revolution after all.

We went by night, unscheduled, to the kroeg. The air which last time had echoed to Whitey's big-talk about who could kill the most kaffirs was now full of decent discussion and welcome to us and not least to Thami Moore and Louis Ndlovu, the sound men. We went to the silo. Did you know that Bloemhof has the biggest silo between somewhere and somewhere else? Probably not. Also that it has the longest dam wall between ditto and ditto. Also that it has more churches per white head than anywhere north of somewhere. We really got into Bloemhof. Into its facts and figures and feel and all.

Then we met the town council, five of whose six members, including the black (officially 'non-statutory') co-chairman Andrew Hanks, were delighted to invite us to sit in on proceedings. Fine, nice new transparent spirit. Hunky-dory. Until the sixth member, the white co-chairman, arrived late and reversed this decision with extreme officiousness and in total absence of consultation with his non-statutory counterpart. I lost my temper and went outside to grouch to the camera with the council building as backdrop. While I was there a door slid cautiously open and there was Hanks, eyes darting furtively like a schoolboy sneaking out of detention, come to whisper apologies. And to think that when he finally rebels and goes bananas the whites are going to say 'now, now, be rational'.

I'd taken strongly to Andrew Hanks and to his chief lieutenant, an excellent youngster named Tuna. Tuna had last time been a main klipgooier and opstoker, undisguised. This time he was into build the nation and pay the rents and obey the law. Not that he saw the new society as all rising sun and Christmas presents. He had plenty of thoughtful gripes about change made and change unmade, but he said what to this day remains the most powerful single comment ever made on the Trek.

He'd been talking about problems. He'd failed to mention to me that he was about to quit university despite a series of strong passes because his pensioner parents couldn't muster the money, and stuck instead to public difficulties. I said: 'Given all these problems that you identify, has the change been meaningful to you?'

He drew a big breath and said, 'I belong.' In print, like this, that looks like not much. But there you have the pallor of print versus the trenchancy the box can produce. The way Tuna said it, deep, rolling, erupting from the depths of his history, half smiling and half daring ... ag, Tuna, you're one of those people who make this nation so exciting.

With Hanks and Tuna and several other local leaders we visited the township administrator, one Van Zyl. Two years previously Tuna had been stoning the administrator's car and nearly all the people I was with would have been arrested the moment they approached the police cordon around the admin compound. This time, greetings and introductions and eyes glazed over while Van Zyl let loose with a torrent of inaudible upbeat statistics about how much was going right.

We met a guy born Ishmail Haffajee and known to mankind as Styles, in honour of his clothing shop into which a live piglet was thrown during the conflict period. We met the pig-thrower, all apologetic and bygones-be-bygones, and we met the pig, piglet no more but now a giant super-beast, kept on permanent semi-show because of its unique role in history. The pig had moreover been named after Styles, in a gesture which the owner apparently genuinely saw as an expression of contrition. Styles, every bit as Muslim as his real name suggests, was not at all sure.

We cut this stuff together all the wrong way. At least, that's obvious in hindsight. It wasn't at the time, it never is. But however wrong the way might have been, the Bloemhof ice-breaker showed me two important things with resounding clarity. First: that to be getting paid to wander around the nation as a sociological sightseer I must have done something right in some previous incarnation. Second: that we'd never do it right in this one.

Viewers would seldom know what wasn't in the programme. I always would. I wanted to get into some of the crunch bits. Yes, it was fine and well that everybody loved one another now, but howcome the actual power-bearing black representation consisted of a single Indian trader from another town? Yes, it was nice that there was an effort going into upgrading the township, but what actual concrete movement was coming from the township itself? Television, I was beginning to learn, is the perfect medium for impact; a dashed lousy one for the conveyance of intelligence.

Faults and all, came the next Tuesday night and Bloemhof was on the screen. It was on urban screens anyway; not on Bloemhof's, NNTV's 'footprint' being an attenuated one. Nevertheless the show was on the road.

5

Censorship and Saint Tau

If I had five bob for every time I've been asked how much the SABC censors us, bank managers would blow fanfares when they saw me coming. The answer is: virtually nil.

Hannatjie Fourie is officially SABC3's 'programme co-ordinator' which de facto includes quality controller. She gets the master copy on, usually, the morning of the day it is to be broadcast. She rings if she particularly likes it, which is about one in three, and she rings if she has a problem, which is so far one in fifteen comma three recurring.

Problem one was the very first programme. In a conversation in Afrikaans I had said 'O Here'. I hadn't thought twice of it. In English I avoid flinging around gratuitous Gods and Christs, knowing that the flinging hurts some people. In Afrikaans, where the proportion of the hurt is presumably higher, you don't notice the Heres, presumably because the proportion of fling-

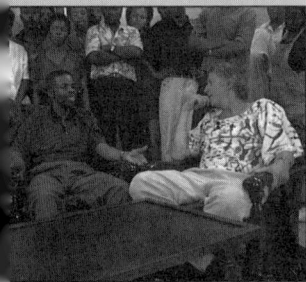

ers is also higher. In the kind of conversations I was having in Bloemhof you would take it as natural that not only Here but also the traditional four-letter words (which are three letters in Afrikaans) would be all over the place (although you also notice that once the camera is rolling the vocabulary changes).

So when Hannatjie phoned to say would we kindly remove the Here, I was surprised. Keith, who never loses his cool, came as close as ever. 'Look,' he said, 'if we're to spend night and day putting this stuff together for the Hannatjie Fouries of the SABC to tell us to take it back, we'd better re-examine this thing.'

Keith at this stage knew no more of Hannatjie than her name, and I could picture the image in his mind: a squeaky airhead peroxide blonde, roots showing through, permanent Stuyvesant lolling from lips, reading 'People' for three quarters of the day and allocating the other quarter to messing producers around.

I had met Hannatjie and already knew better — a tough, smart and very industrious operator, who would always take our side unless there was some compelling reason not to. In not a long time we were to settle in to a thoroughly sound relationship, but that first 'Here' nearly blew the ship out of the water.

Then there was the matter of the 702 shirt.

In Rustenburg the name of a Mr Peter Tau had shot to rapid and extreme prominence. Tau was the chairman of an investment company called Sun Multiserve, which promised high interest rates, if 'high' is an adequate word for 300% in 6 weeks.

The naked nose could smell at a thousand yards that Sun Multiserve was a pyramid scheme. In itself, that was nothing new. The pyramid rip-off is a long ignoble South African tradition, like the Kruger Millions, which keeps finding fresh suckers no matter how loud the past suckers squawk and shriek.

But this was a different pyramid scheme: it was black. Black owned, black run, black initiative and all, which was intriguing.

In a funny way it represented a maturing. Hitherto, blacks had been only among the financial cannon fodder in the get-rich-quick scams. Why shouldn't they be among the instant millionaires as well, and the semi-instant jailbirds?

From a distance I developed a sneaking admiration for the shadowy Mr Tau. He was getting in on the white man's act, and all by himself, no committees, no commissions, no affirmative action quotas. He had just upped and tilted an entrepreneurial lance at his windmill, precisely as I was constantly urging black South Africans to do. True, the lances I had in mind were more in the nature of industry and service and the creation of all-round wealth, but the tilting was so sparse and so feeble that one had to grant a grudging admiration to signs of get-up-and-go wheresoever they were to be found.

Tau's get-up-and-go had netted him something of the order of R50 million in less than half a year and I gather that when people have that much to protect they develop an alacritous trigger finger. Logically it should be the reverse. The more you've got the more relaxed you ought to be, because the proportion you can lose without going broke is so much higher. But logic and human nature cross paths only here and there, and I suspected that Mr Tau's premises might be neither there nor here.

I heard about remonstrations visited by Tau and friends upon sceptics, particularly white ones, and extra-particularly white ones who failed to follow the company's explanation that this was an RDP project, and for the occasion we inspanned an extra crew member to complement the regular team of Richard or Andy plus Louis Ndlovu and Joe Dlamini.

This was Happy Nkhoma, an old friend of mine who had followed an original career path from farm boy to micro-biologist to pharmacist to journalist to marketing manager, and who did odd jobs for me ranging from selling ties to writing articles.

Not that Happy had a gun in a shoulder holster, or a gun anywhere, or even a karate diploma, but he had plenty of Tswana and the fastest mouth in the west, and I figured that if the heavies were to lug us round de back o' de gym it could be handy to have a self-starting vernacular voice available.

Joe and Louis, it should be said, were the most perfect gentlemen and nicest colleagues and decentest companions, but would not see themselves as part of the leadership team. On normal shoots the Trek could have been the Voortrekkers' Trek — the whiteys figuring out the what-now and where-next, and the disenfranchised obligingly observing the ritual of token consultation:

Voice from front seat: 'Guys, okay if we push on to Rooipensdoringdiepfonteinwelverdiendspruit before we think of breakfast?'

Voice from middle seat: 'Yes.'

Voice from rear seat: 'Yes.'

As for actual operating decisions — who to shoot, what question to ask of whom — for a long while I tried the proper and correct quality-circle style thing, ask for ideas, act upon the good ones, let the bad ones down gently. I stopped, in the end, and figured I'd learnt something worthwhile, which the nation was going to spend a long time learning: use the horse for the course, and cease to assume that inside every melamined pigment there is an exec waiting to break out.

Some people belong working out what to do. Some people belong being told to do what the workers-out have worked out for them to do. The distinction has little to do with education or, usually, qualifications, and less to do with complexion. It's a person to person thing, but unfortunately our group-obsessed nation is not a whit less group-obsessed now that groups are constitutionalised out of existence than it was when groups were the compulsory boom of the social mainsail. Then the big thing was 'he's black so he can't be an exec'. Now it is 'he's black so he'd better be an exec'.

When Happy was on the ride, the dynamics were marvellous. A touch hectic from time to time, as bright ideas tumbled forth in chaotic profusion, but inspiringly hectic. Happy would have a firm view on everything from whether we were going to the right place and seeing the right people in the right way at the right time to whether the driver (Richard, Joe, or sometimes me) was on top of *his* job to whether the presenter (me, me, or me) was on top of his job. There were times I was tempted to administer a short jab, and more times that I could see Richard struggling to keep his lip buttoned, but the irritations were outweighed a ton to a penny by the rewards. Happy was a card-carrying member of the working-it-out team, and, like Peter Tau, not by stretch or charity or quota, but by headpower.

After only three or four Fs in the brains test that is Rustenburg's maze of one-way roads, we made it to Multi-serve's head office, in a bank building on the ex-white side of town. The crew were firmly directed to a seat in the large barren reception area. I was firmly escorted through a fierce iron grille and down a passage out of sight. So there was Murphy's law again – my protective vernacular mouth occupied in pleasantries with the receptionists while I had been lured to the belly of the beast.

In a large scruffy boardroom, vast new wood table and matching chairs, I was civilly if coolly received by about thirty people with an average age of ±25 and an average ring-count of about the same. These were sharp dudes with spending money. But for their decorations they would have looked like a Sasco conference.

Each in turn exercised his democratic right to ask me the same question: why was I here and what was I wanting to show. I embellished the answers here and there for the sake of the spice of life, but the thrust was my usual: truth. And no, I was not sent by the Standard Bank, or even United.

After a while thaw took place, as thaw tends to do around tables, and they started enquiring about aspects of various recent Treks. Eventually we were all cackling away happily and it was largely with an eye to the limited life of the daylight that I finally said: 'Well, er, now perhaps I could meet Mr Tau.'

This was somehow some bad thing to say. Suddenly the mood was different and there was mega-discussion in Tswana of which I understood not even the 5% gist that I might have managed in Zulu.

After a few minutes discussion abruptly ceased and the entire party moved off, collecting the crew as we went. It was all very cloak-and-dagger. With much shunting and reversing and clogging of streets a convoy of several cars formed up and we were instructed to follow it. I assumed we were headed for some distant fastness where we were to be admitted to the Presence of the Master. We had hardly started driving when we stopped again and went through the copious rigmarole of re-parking. We were escorted up another set of stairs to a cavernous room full of heavy iron bars like the hall of Pretoria Central.

A hundred or more people were milling about. Still deeply in the dark we joined the milling for a mystifyingly long time. Finally, and in response to no visible change of circumstance or personnel, one of the young guys who had been with us for the two hours odd that had now elapsed abruptly said, 'I'm Peter Tau. I can give you fifteen minutes.'

Apparently this had all been some screening procedure, as seen at the matinées. What it had delivered beyond effluxion of time was hard to see, but there was a passmark at hand. Maybe it had involved spirit mediums. Tau barked an order. Two low lounge chairs materialised in the middle of the hall. Tau and I sat, our heads at waist level among the throng of standing bodies, and he set out his case.

As he portrayed it, he was a latter-day black man's messiah. He had been a miner (earning, I supposed, about as much per annum as he was currently making per minute) when he realised that he had a calling to restore the wealth of the African people. So he had set up Multiserve, which was admirably meeting this need and would have gone on to enrich the entire country had it not been that the white bankers were jealous and had sabotaged it.

I knew that the banks did not see matters precisely the same way. By their logic a pyramid scheme inevitably ends up in tears, the quantity of tears depending directly on how long it goes on.

The essence of the pyramid is that I the investor earn my return by virtue of how many second-generation investors I bring in behind me. I give you, say, R100. I then persuade four more people to give you R100 each. Out of that R400 you give me R200 and you keep R200. Each of the four new investors brings in a further four. Out of that R1 600 you pay out 4 × R200 to four newly happy investors, and another R200 to me, now the grandfather investor, and you keep R600. The next generation brings in R6 400 and pays out maybe R4 000, and so it goes on even unto the fifth and tenth and twentieth generation, by which time you need industrial-strength calculators to keep tally of your earnings and Fort Knox to stash your cash.

You may have heard the nice apocryphal tale about the workman who did a month-long job for one of the Caesars, and said to Caesar: 'This should be a task worth a thousand denarii, but if you would care to just give me one denarius on the first day and then double it every day for the month, that'd be okay by me.'

The story goes that Caesar leapt at the prospect of stealing a march on this dumb simpleton and said 'sure'; so that a month later he'd laid out twenty-one million denarii. (Unless perhaps the month was February.)

That's why pyramid schemes can't work. There aren't enough people in the nation or the world to sustain them into even the middle term, let alone long. The crash is built in. The only question is when the crash and how it comes. In this case the banks had blown the whistle at the point of 53 000 investors, meaning that the howls of outrage amounted to a pretty fierce wind but something less than a tornado. Another month, you could have had five or ten million angry blacks saying look what the whites have done to us this time.

However, it is a little hard to explain the flaw at the core of the system to a guy whose dreams the system has just turned real. The critical faculties wither or evaporate under enough material pressure. Years ago I knew a lawyer, a very strait-laced upright guy, church every Christmas and Easter without fail, Michaelhouse and Bryanston, never used the salad fork for dessert or tilted the soup plate the wrong way. This guy had been upper crust since before he was born, and he got into a pyramid scheme based on cosmetics. He'd already made a small fortune and was on his way to a big fortune, for part of which I was meant to be one of his incoming 'distributors'. I refused on the grounds that while I might make what he said I'd make, it was going to come from some ancient sukkeling pensioner a little further down the line, already cold and hungry and about to end up ruined. My lawyer friend couldn't believe it. He had mastered the law of contract. He could assemble appliance kits imported from Japan. He was in the top intellectual bracket. But put to him the simple logical proposition that his new Mercedes was taking vitamins out of the mouth of some benighted township baby, and this was Greek.

Same with Tau's hundred acolytes, who chimed in cacophonously to enumerate the goodies that Father Christmas in the chair next to me had provided. Typically they had gone up in 300% steps, and some of them many steps. From R400, the usual opening bid, some now had R12 000 and R15 000 locked up because of the white man's jealousy, *as well* as having new houses, new cars, new furniture and, in some cases, something with which to have at last paid the school fees.

Various of these guys took us to see the new houses and new furniture, and the day became difficult. Here were humble people with slow sad eyes looking at me in horror. How could I fail to rejoice with them, that where they had had a corner of their grandmother's bathroom to live in they now had a neat whole house with quadrophonic sound?

After a long line of cosy new urban homes (not one of them in the township — everybody heading for ex-white territory) I had seen the point. I had also established that Peter Tau wears not merely a halo in the eyes of his peers, but wings and orb and sceptre as well and probably a long white beard. I had also become yet again amazed by the smoothness with which small-town Afrikanerdom had adjusted to the new world.

These were the kind of Boere who ride to the factory on an old black bicycle. They were supposed to be agitated about their neighbourhood disappearing from them. But we were finding ourselves in neighbourhoods where the whites were now 10% and 20%, and they were waving and greeting as insouciantly as you like — schoolkids, tannies, the lot. I wouldn't bet on the same reaction when the liberals are outnumbered by the darkies. It was fine to be gung ho against apartheid when you imagined maybe one black doctor per suburb. When it becomes five black doctors per street, and some of them have very wobbly doctorates, and all of them have lots of cousins who stay over on long visits that they spend roaming about, it's a different matter, even before the first bold soul gets round to a ritual slaughter on the front lawn. Or a Friday to Wednesday stokvel for 700 guests from the township.

That the Boere embraced Africa so much tighter than the Engelse did is a continuing miracle, but is not without its logic. The Boere, bear in mind, spent 342 years believing that when eventually the dread day happened that 'the blacks take over' the sun would snuff it and hell be born on earth. When they ended up with an incredibly dignified gentleman in a No 6 rugby jersey they couldn't believe their luck. The contrast between reality and expectation was a millennial relief.

The liberals had expected the new society to doff a grateful hat in their direction, and knock politely at their door for advice on how to run things properly. What they got was personally hijacked and politically ignored. No wonder they turned cantankerous.

But whilst the sights and sounds of transformation in Rustenburg were fascinating, a sameness crept in. One new shiny CD player looks much the same as the next. A neat new two-bedroom klinker-brick is not that different from a neat new two-bedroom plaster-and-paint. And every time I'd come to the core question with the proud householders – 'excuse me, but you do realise your new-found prosperity rests upon the losses of someone further down the chain' – I'd be answered by a blankness so total that I might have been talking nuclear physics.

I wanted something different in some way, even if just visual. I asked if there was a rural village somewhere nearby, where people had views on the matter. Ah yes, I was confidently told, right close by.

Well, we arrived at this close-by village, Kana, a little before nightfall, and I do believe we were still the right side of the equator. I was travel-weary and day-weary and unimpressed, but to this day Mme Megoe is one of the vividest memories I have from the hundreds of places we went to in the course of the Trek.

Mme Megoe, Mme meaning Mrs and Megoe pronounced Mech-weh, had formerly been a domestic servant right there in Parkview, my own suburb of Johannesburg, and had now retired here to the sticks where like an answer to a prayer Mr Tau had come along in a flaming chariot to make her rich. All that she could not understand was why the white peoples wanted her to be poor again. Why did it worry the white peoples that now she could pay for the borehole to be fixed, that now she had bought the bricks — look, those ones there — for the new kitchen? Her only sadness was that God had given the white peoples bad hearts. For all her life she had been defending the white peoples, and saying no they can be good peoples, even peoples who can help us when our own peoples behave wrong, but now, tch, this jealousy by the white peoples against her bricks was just too much. Did the white peoples not understand there was no other way she could make money here in the bundus?

Well, yes. That was what was driving this particular white people crazy. Mme Megoe's place was something from a storybook. This was idyllic rural Africa at its spirit-lifting best. This little old lady had maybe an acre, maybe a hectare, of land, land that after the great rains of early '96 was temporarily as green and lush as a Northumberland garden. The homestead consisted of six or eight semi-adjoined units, as scrubbed and polished and tidy as is to be had. The grass was rich, the crops were high, a wild abundance of fruit trees was everywhere. We sat under an ancient gnarled vine at a corner of the expansive stoep, and we ate pomegranates.

The last pomegranate I ate was in some previous incarnation. You don't find them laid out among the grapes and pawpaw slices at the end of a dinner, perhaps because they're messy bastards to slurp. You don't even come across them at the greengrocer much; I'd love to know why. I sat under the vine, pomegranate juice trickling from my cheeks and chin all over my clothes, and felt like a king.

A frustrated king. This was how Africa was supposed to be: warm hospitality, warm people, vibrant nature all about. And this was how Mme Megoe could be making a real living, a value-adding living instead of a sleight-of-hand living, for not only herself but for others in the village — employees, suppliers, spin-off contractors...

She could be running a bed-and-breakfast. For a certain kind of tourist, local as well as outsider, she'd be a stand-out. She could offer more than an overnight pillow; she could offer a slice of Africa. Her granddaughters could handle the cooking and the waitressing, and double the Gross Village Product from a single appreciative German or American tip. Her neighbour could give the once-over to the old cart standing in his yard, and feed up the couple of nags grazing from the streetside and offer a half-day tour of the environs. The shebeen down the road might do some creative thinking regarding evening entertainment. The local craftsmen could acquire the beginnings of a local market.

Basking in the evening sun, developing the rudiments of ingesting pomegranates with approximate grace, I found it mouth-watering to let the mind run loose on how tourism could transform the life of Kana.

Unfortunately, running loose is about all that's going to happen. Who the hell is there to organise and promote and sustain a venture like that? You'd like to think some local entrepreneur could get things going, but you know that if you raised it with the locals the best you'd get is a lot of long looks. Maybe somebody would say: if this is such a good idea why isn't the government doing it?

On white farms and in white villages the B&B industry is proceeding apace. Ten years ago it consisted of an occasional resentful tannie who would show you to the room vacated by her son in the army, his boots under the bed and his pin-ups on the wall. You'd share a bathroom with the five daughters and your breakfast would be soggy scrambled eggs with limp bacon, eaten under the suspicious eyes of the family ensuring that their horrible china ornaments do not accidentally leap into your pockets. B&B was a desperation resort for travellers who couldn't afford a hotel. Nowadays you have effort in the business, and profits in it. What you don't have in it is Africans. The B&B register shows a monolithic list of white names making white money while the blacks look on and say you white peoples are doing us down.

After Mme Megoe the day was out and so was our energy, but we'd been told a lot about copy-cat get-rich-quick schemes that had mushroomed in Multiserve's wake. We'd also been told, several times, that some of these were run by whites and that these ones had been allowed to continue uninterrupted. I was 99% willing to bet that this claim was paranoia, but the 1% niggled. Moreover I was jolted by a fellow who pulled out two sets of deposit slips and said: 'Look, this one is for Multiserve. You see there I deposited R1 200 and you see here I was paid out R3 600. This one is from the white company: you see here I deposited R720 and you see here they have written "sorry dividends delayed by lack of funds". Now can you explain to me why Multiserve's accounts are frozen but the white company is still receiving new deposits?'

We had to come back to look at this stuff, and the next morning, bleary and half asleep in the pre-dawn, it happened that the shirt I pulled out of the cupboard was a very distinctive one: '702 election coverage '94', it read. 'We made it up as we went along.'

At Rustenburg, Richard was gearing up the camera and I was about to march into a long grim black hole filled with aspirant windfall-winners from a Multiserve lookalike when Richard noticed the shirt and rang the alarm.

I said: 'Nah, nobody's that petty-minded.'

Richard said: 'Maybe turn it inside out just in case.'

I did, to the amusement of the multitudes waiting for the black hole to open, but it showed through and looked ridiculous and furtive and wrong.

Richard said: 'Let's buy a shirt, just in case,' and we were about to but the black hole was suddenly unbarred and the throng was sucked into it and we didn't want to miss, so the rest of the day was in the 702 shirt.

The rest of the day had assorted worthwhile bits, including a fair amount of evidence on the terrific colour-coding of not only this issue but also the general worldview of the black citizenry of

Rustenburg when the chips were down. (It also involved a considerable withering of the idea that white rip-off schemes were deliberately left in action.) However, there was only one bit which it seriously pained my soul to forfeit, which was a friendly fellow walking with me along a street and earnestly explaining: 'The only problem is that white people read too many books and therefore you don't understand. You tell me it is impossible for the scheme to work, but I see that every time I give them R400 they give me back R1 200, so I know better than your books.'

The upshot was: Hannatjie phoned about the shirt. 'Oh, c'mon, Hannatjie,' I said, 'this is beneath you. 702 doesn't worry when somebody phones there about my TV show. Let it be.'

Hannatjie said: 'You don't understand. There's been a huge fuss here about people sneaking in skelm ads.' She explained: for example, in a soapie you suddenly have a surprisingly extended shot of a lounge suite, and then a sort of accidental close-up on the manufacturer's name. This stuff had been going too far, and now there was a big thing about cutting it out entirely.

I could understand that. I'd been amazed by how they got away with it. But I was so righteous in my own innocence that I was indignant at the notion that anyone could think I would do a similar shooftie deal with anyone, shy little retiring 702 or anyone.

As the cliché says, some you win and some you lose. I went so far as a direct appeal to Louis who, after reinforcing all that Hannatjie had said, wisely concluded with 'in that light, I leave it to you'. So I wasn't being censored; I wasn't being bullied or commanded; I had to make my own decision, just with one small factor to take into account; whether every possible viewer of this programme was going to be as fully aware as I was that the 702 shirt was a matter of an innocent freedom, having nothing whatsoever in common with the close-ups on the lounge suites.

A day's worth of shooting got left out of the Multiserve programme (which meant relief for the editors, who for once had a mere half-gallon to cram into a pint pot) and that was the second of the three times that the SABC worried vocally about anything we did. The third and last was when we got into Affirmative Action. That programme, as I explain later, was bedevilled by factors that could have been — wrongly — laid at the feet of the black company which produced it. Hannatjie, very decently, gave me a thorough grilling to ensure that this company was getting a square deal. They were, and she accepted my assurances to that effect.

The overall point is that my experience with the SABC is a rebuttal of one of the standard grouches about the corporation: the grouch that says 'everything is totally controlled, nobody is allowed to say anything out of line'. I say out-of-line things every week, and nearly every week the ratings are higher than the week before (among black viewers somewhat more conspicuously than white). If anyone at the SABC is agitated about the line, it hasn't come to my ears.

I don't think my show is anywhere near to Ultimate Television. I do think that its continuance reflects a degree of freedom of the airwaves, a freedom widely disregarded by the self-consciously sophisticated critics who say 'there's nothing on the SABC; the only thing worth watching is the BBC'. Junk, people. The BBC might indeed do it better, but we do it here.

6
Impact and its Price

Plettenberg Bay is not so much a geographic entity as — I steal from Sarah Britten — 'a set of co-ordinates in the popular imagination'. Plettenberg Bay *stands* for things, things that according to your position within the popular imagination you might articulate either as grace and elegance and the values that make life civilised, or, particularly during exposure to the supercilious supremacist raucous rantings of tipsy socialites with rocks on their fingers and rocks in their heads, as a compelling case for a dose of serious Stalinism.

Plettenberg Bay is not a place to harmlessly drop into any old conversation. If you spend Christmas at Umhlanga or Muizenberg or Southbroom or Philippolis you can say so with impunity. It's orrait. If at Plettenberg Bay, you get sensitive. In some kinds of company you may care to slip it in ever so gently and let it clang on its own, like a falling barbell. 'Mm, Port Edward?

Very nice, I believe. Uh, we were at Plett.' In other company you may be less keen to shove your name into the kaleidoscope of Plett images that convey excess and sharp practice and hubris and complacency and onanistic Sandton 4x4s that remain forever virgin of a dirt road.

It is in the consequent spirit of ambivalence that I tell you that we stayed last summer with friends at Keurbooms, which shares a beach with a better known neighbouring locality. At the beach in question, viz Lookout, we came across a guy from the American programme Sixty Minutes.

This guy was — and if memory is not exact my figures are at least in the ball park — one of the 13 *British* staff of Sixty Minutes. In America there were something like 196 staffers, and around the world were numerous agents and contractors on an infinite range of strings. The guy described how there'd be a meeting in January to work out July's programmes, whereafter a flow system like a rocket launch swung into being. By the time it all happened, the producers would know at what time of day which conversation was going to take place; what coffee table would be positioned in which corner of the lounge with how many flowers on it in which colours; who was going to say what, with how long a pause between sentences and what interjections at what point.

This, I guess, was the American way of doing things. That was why they were big and rich and could resell their programmes to thousands of TV channels all around the world, thereby getting constantly bigger and richer while the rest of us come to see it as axiomatic that we know more about American scandals than our own scandals and more about the life of the black American gentry than the life of our own rainbow compatriots.

On one level I envied this scale, imagining that if we could do it with 50 or 100 times the budget we would produce a programme with 50 or 100 times the calibre. On another level, I wondered. Let alone that *that* much order and system would upset my stomach, it is arguable that the hectic chaos of our week-by-week delivery produced more spontaneity and thus perhaps more authenticity.

There were times that the word 'spontaneity' was less close to mind than the word 'frenzy'. Take the time we were hurtling across the Kalahari to Upington airport. We needed a wrap — a closing statement to a programme on the area. We needed it *in* the area. We wanted it in a setting that made sense. The map indicated that the Augrabies Falls were but a couple of kilometres off the main road. We took the turn, gauging to the minute how long we could be and how fast the remaining drive would be. What the map hadn't indicated was that there would be queues and delays and tickets, and that the parking lot was a health-giving walk from the falls. We ran across those rocks like the devil was close behind. Richard Burnett shot the wrap from the shoulder, with chest heaving like no cameraman is allowed to heave. I panted out my summing-up at nineteen to the dozen. I habitually talk too fast anyway. This one, I might have been aiming for the record books. There were flies in my eyes, too, not to mention nose, mouth, ears, shirt and underpants. We were in the middle of a fly thicket. By the time we hit the airport — and ran again for the plane — we were anti-social globules of congealed sweat and fly purée.

Take our day at Pretoria Central Prison — one of the two occasions that we shot a whole programme in a single day. We had about nine hours of footage that day, and it was a day of such a nature that had our programme been three hours long we could have filled it without a worry.

Beforehand I had been lukewarm about doing prisons; it was well-travelled territory. Afterwards I felt differently, and, I was surprised to find, extremely emotional. I spent half the day as 'a warder' and the other half as 'a prisoner', and I came away Damascusly converted to a previously unsuspected view on crime and punishment.

Yes, yes, like everybody says we need real deterrents against the crime wave. It's doubtless true that there are a lot of people outside who ought to be in. But I had not dimly glimpsed the opposite truth: there are a lot of people inside who ought to be out. There are people in there to whom the being in is no longer of any value whatsoever to anyone.

The public instinct — 'oh, criminals' — is understandably less than brimful of compassion (and much less compassionate than many of the warders I met). I had pretty much shared the instinct until my brief time inside introduced me to the immense variety of human beings suppressed beneath the 'criminal' sobriquet. Some of them, I shudder in relief that they are in no position to meet me in an alley one night. Others leave me feeling strongly aware of how far the world has yet to go in making sense of punishment. Nor do only my bleeding-heart liberal eyes see that way. I was taken aback by the number of Correctional Services people, often of humble rank, who had tales to tell of how Prisoner A or Prisoner B remained in jail solely because even the newly flexible system is not flexible enough to see that the remaining is tragically pointless.

By the time the officers chucked me out — they wouldn't let me stay overnight — I was physically exhausted, emotionally hammered and intellectually punch-drunk. All I knew was that when they asked if I wanted to lock the place up — I had done the 'ontmeestering', the preliminary unlocking round with the master-key in the morning — the answer was a No Thanks. In a crowded prison corridor, with the officers pointedly rattling their key-rings and clearing their throats, I tried to explain to the camera why not.

The explanation was not a jewel of lucidity. Peter Wilhelm in the Financial Mail took the trouble to transcribe it, and the liberty to transcribe it phonetically, and when you read his account, in one non-stop paragraph, it looks like gibberish. Maybe it was gibberish. It certainly wouldn't do for Sixty Minutes. Then again, in the finished programme we cut from this scene to the prison choir singing about going home to their heavenly father, while the credits rolled down the screen, and of all the Treks we did this was the only one to which people routinely respond by saying: 'I cried.'

I don't mind them crying. I did some crying myself, truth be told. I might have been wrong on everything else, but I'm not wrong on the core proposition that the retribution industry is still floundering in the Dark Ages. You cry now, maybe you think later. More likely than if you yawn and stretch and zap the remote and say, 'supper ready yet, darling?' More likely even than if you say, 'wow that was a very professionally produced programme'. I'll live without Sixty Minutes' trappings.

The bigger trouble than the shooting was the putting it together. We'd go somewhere; we'd love being there; we'd revel in the people we met; I'd be driven scatty by the vast quantity of broadcastable comments and expressions and interchanges that happened off camera; we'd come back with maybe six or eight hours of footage to process into an allegedly comprehensible half-hour. Yo.

Several times the SABC changed our slot. Usually a change in slot meant a change in duration. We shrank from 45 minutes to 30, and then when NNTV transmogrified into the ads-seeking SABC3, 26 minutes. For good or ill the ads SABC3 was seeking were initially thin on the ground, so we could usually stretch the 26 minutes to 28 and save a few hours of agony in the edit suite.

You've probably heard the speechifying story variously ascribed to Churchill, Shaw, Kissinger, and maybe by now Mandela too:

'Oh Mr X, how long does it take to prepare a speech?'

'Depends. A one hour speech you stand up and speak, a half-hour you spend a half-hour preparing, and a 10-minuter takes an hour.'

The same principle applies to written work. You can make a point in 1 000 words in half the time you can make the same point in 800 words; say nothing of 500. But the terrors of refining the written word are as nought to the terrors of tweaking the moving image.

In print, you only have one thing to worry about: content. If Point X is a point you earnestly want in, you get it in. You shove, push, pull, stretch, cram, bend, press, squeeze, scratch and bite until your words shriek for mercy, but if you try hard enough you get it in. You might have thought it was a classy and rounded point in four leisurely sentences, and you will harden your heart to its pitiful cries as the sentences lose their class, and their rounding, and then become three, and two and finally all too possibly a terse staccato telegram that perplexes the reader more than if you'd given up to start with, but, and this is the nub, if you want it in you can get it in. If there's a nuance, there's a subtlety, that you believe is better hinted at than ducked . . . subject solely to patience, anybody can edit any piece of written copy so that at least in theory it touches on all of the bits you want and wastes not a millimetre on what you don't want.

TV, nope. Whereas abundant time could solve many of the flaws posed by our brand of woeful time, the happy state of notional perfection is not available, even in theory. It is disposed of by the vicious triangle of content, visual, and audio, and further ravaged by the necessary fight that the content-minded presenter is bound to have with his video-minded editor, who must and will fight with knuckledusters and rabbit-punches at every attempt you make to compromise the impact on the eye or the impact on the ear for the sake of message.

If you think I'm overstating, good luck to you and please pass my regards to the Easter Bunny. That is how TV works. The industry is built around the one-liner: the crack, the quip, the cry of rage; and around the instant image, the falling tear, the gnarled forehead wreathed in touching smiles. Unless you have a captive audience, such as Std 8 mathematics, you can't lecture the screen. Nor can you feed it the kind of conversation which would induce the viewer, happening upon the same conversation at his local kroeg, to drum his fingers and cast his eyes around for who might be telling barcounter jokes. Give the box a comment of longer than around 90 seconds, and you can palpably feel it wilt.

The box is never comfortable as a debating chamber, and with all due respect (that smarmy phrase with which lawyers preface their put-downs) you cannot validly tell me: 'Nonsense, look at all the debates we see on TV.' Ask yourself what actual point of substance you remember from a TV debate.

Debate on TV is not like debate in real life, and not like print debate either. Real life you listen, or *can* listen. Print you imbibe, and if you are keen enough you can imbibe quite a lot; you re-read, you cogitate, you go back to paragraph ii and reconsider point xi. TV debate is public spectacle, doing for the Twentieth Century what the Roman circus did for the Noughth Century. A big-time debate means a debate with big-time figures involved. What the viewers tune in for is the figures, not the content, and from tomorrow morning until the twilight of time the echoes will be personal echoes: who wore red socks; who had a squiff hairpiece or a big gap tooth; who lost his rag; who got sulky.

I bet you remember — when was it? '92? — how Mandela reached over and shook De Klerk's hand. I bet you have not the faintest idea what that debate was about. I'm sure you remember Buthelezi busting into the Durban studio with his swaggerstick; about 3 minutes on air. I greatly doubt (with respect) that you have much of a handle on Buthelezi's copious and comprehensive restatements of his worries re the federal form of State; interminable hours on air. (And if you do have that handle you got it more from what you read than from what you saw. You're by definition a reader, after all, or what are you doing on this page?)

TV's scorecard is simple. Impact 1; Content 0. I sound like an ingrate, no doubt; a traitor to the TV cause. Should I be remorseful, and grovel for forgiveness? No way. My heart pumps custard, which is a lot more than TV's heart pumps. TV is ironclad, and it laughs off the pinpricks of trivial cavil. What is more, its laugh is the laugh of the way to the bank. Who needs content when you can have that impact? And nothing else comes even within spitting distance of the impact.

Maybe it's obvious, but to me it is light years more obvious now that I have served stints of multiple years in each of the three core media: for the conveyance of intelligence (in the 'military intelligence' sense, meaning 'information-plus') TV gets 2 out of 10, radio about 5 or 6, and print can get right up to 9,999. In respect of impact, it's diametrically opposite, and worse.

Print, you can wrestle through the small hours, battling mightily for the word, the phrase, the point that gets it right. And you cast your bread unto the waters, and yea, verily, it disappeareth even like dew in the Namib. On TV you can take ten unplanned seconds and utter a tenth or twentieth of that point, angry that the other nine or nineteen parts get lost on the way, and over months and years to come you can be staggered — and sometimes very seriously humbled — to realise that you have changed the nation's thinking. Of course I mean 'change' by the tiniest fraction of the tiniest millimetre, change that to an outside eye would look pathetic. But when people walk up to you and say: 'Hey, you made me think differently', that's daunting, no matter how fine a micro-difference it may be.

Take the matter of squatters and squalor. Once upon a time I had laboured under the standard middle-class belief that squatters = misery + threat + skrik. This had changed with acquaintance. I got to know that some squatter camps could be a thousand times more habitable than others, and indeed encouraging nuclei of urban life.

Unfortunately the distinction usually lies in the degree of strong-armedness of the local tyrant and his henchmen, who in the current fashion often quaintly call themselves 'Mayor and

Committee'. I don't suppose that on the whole the squatter strongmen qualify as paragons of kindliness, but then again they have also been known to be very useful local leaders — initiating schooling, creating streets and parks and minimum property sizes and maximum densities, ensuring that households equip themselves with rubbish pits and toilet pits, and so on. The methods of enforcement do not necessarily pay due care and attention to the human rights clauses of the constitution, and in general the optimistic side of squatterdom is by no means unflawed. However, that there can be an optimistic side at all is news to your average suburbanite with a bond and a rates assessment, who is dedicated to seeing squatter existence as degradation all the way.

The horrors of horror-story squatting are drastic horrors, but not all squatting is horror-story. Squatter camp can vary from squatter camp as much as the leafy luxury of Saxonwold varies from the compressed crush of Judith's Paarl, and the most liveable squatter camps are in many ways more liveable than many brands of formal housing. Some of those guys are as bourgeois as anybody, with their ducks on the wall and their mantelpiece decorations. Just that they lack an address (which, when you think it over, is an extraordinary thing to lack). To be sure, I'm not offering to swop. I'm not saying I'd like to be a squatter, whether or not with cardboard walls and holes in the roof. I'm not about to relinquish my own bourgeois comforts with title deed and credit rating and all. But a lot of people are not about to acquire those comforts, not in this century and I wonder about the next. The question is whether we the stable and the comfortable do better by treating squatters as a threatening mass or by cultivating hope and humanity where those things are to be found.

Over the years I've written a fair amount on this theme, urging (a) policies that encourage squatters to do their own thing rather than being misled by the belief that government will house them, (b) a downsizing of the panic reaction from the whiteys and, ideally, a bit of constructive engagement.

Both these injunctions might have been in Latin for all they said to my compatriots. True, my compatriots were by no means claiming to avidly devour the Gospel According To Beckett. In fact my magazines, Frontline and later Sidelines, were distinguished by the most exclusive, which is to say minuscule, readerships going. However, even that modest readership, which responded well enough to other recurring themes, completely bypassed the proposition that it could be handy to recognise the potential in squatter life and not only the threat.

But then came the day that we Trekked off to Orange Farm, the 'Squatter Soweto' mushrooming between Johannesburg and Vanderbijlpark, and shared a cold winter's night with Beauty Msimango and a video camera.

Beauty spent much of her time living at my house in Johannesburg, where her fiancé, Billy Modise, was a long-standing fixture of one of those tousled African-style relationships that can work with such special reward. Billy wasn't employed by us, and wasn't a tenant either, at least as in rent-paying. He was just there. He'd moved in twenty years back, and stayed, and he did things for us and we did things for him, and aside from certain concerns raised by Billy's roving eye and the care and maintenance of the offspring thereof, this was your classic win-win arrangement. It was all the better when Beauty pitched up, living up to her name in every way, and took him in hand. Not least, Billy, whose after-sales fatherhood of his own kids was less than unblemished, became a pretty good stepfather to hers.

In time, Beauty wanted her own house. Our garden started to fill up with bricks and window frames and metal sheets, new from hardware shops as well as old from scrap merchants, and one Saturday morning there was an almighty shuffling and kerfuffling up and down the drive in the small hours, and this was Billy having laid on a contractor to lug Beauty's house, in kit form, to Orange Farm.

On the Monday Billy had afterthought supplies to transport, supplies too big for a taxi but not enough to warrant hiring another truck. So I took him, and I was bowled over. There was Beauty's house in considerable picturesque glory, tidy and intact, where two days before there had been bare earth.

Came the weekend and feast time at Kwa-Beauty, and there were five extra guests — myself plus crew.

Some portions of this experience were... uh, uneven. Glossing over the tendency of the first-world suburban rectum to behave obstinately when confronted with a dark and seatless long-drop, there was the fact that our presence brought forth a large contingent of additional neighbours, most of whom were drunk.

In fact the general level of drunkenness was off-putting. I hadn't expected Orange Farm of a Saturday night to feel like a teetotallers'convention but neither had I anticipated that everybody out of doors after dark would be motherless. The only exceptions were Billy and Beauty and a handful of their own party — who of a normal evening would have been very much indoors — and a religious group who were disembowelling a goat for a sangoma's initiation ceremony, and were high on the blood of the goat and the beat of the drums and the mysticism.

Everyone else was out of it, and when everybody you meet is staggering and slurring it gives you a dim impression. You have to consciously recall that this is also a skewed impression precisely for the reason that the other lot, the straight and the sober, are behind locked doors, and even then there is something painful about the relationship between black people and liquor. It's a relationship which is all extremes and no middle.

In circles like mine liquor consumption works in a bell curve — a small number of teetotallers one side, a small number of pisscats the other side, a large number of two-beer or three-glass moderates around the middle. The township pattern is a large number of (understandably disapproving) abstainers on the near side, practically nobody in the middle, and a deluge of hopeless soaks at the far side. I'm not saying that the white custom is any great shakes either, but that if you're going to drink at all (and heaven knows why any of us ever starts) rather drink so that you can stop than drink so that you lose it. When I see young white kids getting into liquor I think that's stupid and mildly risky. I see their black contemporaries starting and think that's tragic.

So the Orange Farm exercise had its down sides, but then it also had ups that went up to the clouds. Beauty and her daughters and the womenfolk had been busy cooking with a little two-plate ministove. Eventually we were called in for supper, which became an awkward moment because by now there were a few dozen drunk hangers-on invoking African custom as their passport to the meal. (A passport which Beauty vehemently refused to recognise.)

Finally there were ten or so of us in the shack, and Beauty delivered a seriously classy dinner. I was sitting on her bed. On the walls were her paintings and decorations. A large china clock in the shape of a cartoon dog dominated the bedside table. There was barely room to breathe but there was grace and small-b beauty and hospitality, and this came across as maybe two minutes on camera, and all the problems I'd always had explaining the optimism of squatter life were no more. From that day to this not a week has gone by that somebody does not say, in a tone of open-mouthed astonishment words to the effect that: 'You know, I'd never realised that the squatter people could be like that.' It was an image. It was a natural for the box.

It was Impact.

Not so the other side of the same Trek: The q. of Housing vs Infrastructure.

74

We went with Dan Mofokeng, the Gauteng MEC for Housing, on a tour of West Rand squattery. I argued that his government's best option was to say: 'Sorry, people, we didn't mean that stuff about building you a million houses in five years. It was a mistake. Build your own, and we'll concentrate on water and sewerage and electricity.'

I was hot on the theme and got hotter on that very trip, especially upon meeting a fellow whose home-made house was a work of art, with wall-papered interiors and a neo-Victorian fireplace and two skylights and a doorbell that played Waltzing Matilda. He shrugged off my awed compliments: 'Ag, it's just an mkhukhu – a shack – I'll pull it down when the government comes to build me a real house.' That's not just one sad delusion but two: that he'll get a 'real house' at all and that it will be superior to the product of his own noble toil.

Dan wasn't buying my case. As to why not, the brass tacks evaded us. We bypassed one another. Dan had lots of politician-speak, which I had difficulty nailing and double difficulty nailing in TVable length. I suppose he had difficulty with my spectator-speak, as people doing a job invariably have when people who are not doing it tell them how to do it better. We didn't come to a resolution or even to clarity on the nature of the argument.

What we did come to was a fellow who snowed our ears about white theft. All whites were thieves, he said, half amusing and half ominous, so would I depart without delay before he lost something. As soon as you saw whites you knew you were going to lose something, and next thing you'd be in debt as well. So whites must just stay away, and never again show him pieces of paper proving that he owes them sums of money he doesn't understand.

It did not pass notice that he had happily let me relieve him of his barrow, heavy and cumbersome under a steel window-frame, for several hundred metres before he embarked on his white-theft tirade.

The feature of any Trek that goes down best is the sight of D Beckett Esq puffing and blundering in the course of performing an improbable task. This one would have been in the top rank, especially when my foot slipped into a mud puddle. Except you couldn't hear a word. On the sound track Mr Theft's barely decipherable English mingled with shouts and laughs and cat-calls and cheers from a hundred bystanders.

The 'intellectual' side of the squatter programme was lost because Dan and I were too long-winded, and a good deal of the gee-whizz side was lost because the local residents had failed to attend elocution lessons or to internalise the desirability of speaking one at a time and close to the microphone. We did broadcast a chunk of the houses-or-drains debate, but I've never yet heard a viewer make a reference to it. TV's impact works only where TV lets it work, like Beauty's banquet and her China poodle.

It's *when* it works that it works like a nuclear bomb.

It worked in Weenen, too, where we went to watch a land war.

Weenen is a dorp in the Natal midlands. Its name means 'weeping', or 'where we cried', or at any rate would mean that but in English nowadays everybody pronounces it 'wee nin' rather than the original 'veer nen'. One feature of Weenen's blood-drenched background — when the Boere weren't bashing the Brits or vice versa, either or both were donnering the Zulus or vice versa — is the split perceptions of the same event. 'Weenen' is what the maps say, but what the Zulus say is 'Kwanobamba', 'the place where we caught them'.

Weenen now faces a divergence of opinion. Nearly all the land belongs to a handful of commercial (ie white) farmers, while hundreds of thousands of Zulus, their numbers increasing by the minute, share a few desolate pockets. Obviously, the proper and rightful response to this unjust state of affairs is 'shame, correction must take place'. That's what I thought from a distance. That's why I connected with Rory Alcock, a striking amalgam of white Zulu, Greek god, and born Irishness, who carries on the work of his famous murdered father, Neil, in speaking up for the landless. That's why when I arrived at the offices of the farmers' Conservancy they treated me like a snake in the chicken hok.

The more we looked, the less of the shame response I felt. Rory escorted us everywhere, introducing the landless aggrieved by the dozen. The more I met, the more hardegat I became. All I heard was people saying 'give us more land' and all I saw was the ruination of the land they already had. The low point was when Rory took us to The Chief's Field, the communal farmland administered by the Chief in the common good.

The Chief's Field was a chunk of land of ... I don't know, maybe 50 hectares, maybe 200; a big chunk, I'm getting at, not a 'field' as in rugby field or cricket field, and alongside the river daarby. It was irrigated. It was a mess. Even where we stood the irrigators were spraying away fit to burst. What they were spraying was the blackjacks. The whole field was one vast mess of blackjacks, except for a single distant chunk that was green and lush and ordered. This chunk was leased out to a Mr Van Breda.

Rory had the usual sociological explanations-cum-excuses for this pathetic state of affairs. I'd had a couple of years too many hearing the excuses, and was hard about it. Add to it the general hopelessness of what the Zulus were telling me on all sides, and the overall picture was not encouraging.

One fellow, on the middle of an erosion-ravaged hill getting more eroded even under our eyes, told me about all the things that it was necessary for the government, or someone, to supply.

I asked if he wasn't able to dig contours in the meanwhile?

He said that the people had 'just' acquired the 'green light of knowledge' about contours, and would be going at it forthwith. The way he talked was as if this arcane bit of knowledge had been kept secret until last night, and the people were this very moment off collecting shovels. But I knew that if I came back in six months or a year or five years it'd be the same.

Another fellow was cross that things were no longer like they had been before the white man came, when every adult male had a hill to himself. That dispensation, he said, had to be restored. That was it; the solution. Final. I said, no, hang on, there were maybe 50 000 people then where there are 5 000 000 now. The guy scratched his head as if I was talking trigonometry, and simply repeated, per interpreter, his same grievance: before the whites, everything was zinhle.

Someone else's grandfather had been evicted from a farm after decades of service and alleged centuries of prior occupancy. This chap vehemently demanded the descendants' right to live where his grandfather had lived. It turned out there had been eleven sons, each with an average of eleven sons, most of whom had families. They all had to go back to the farm. In the face of this kind of logic, I find that human compassion turns to stone. When a farmer kicks an aged retired retainer out of the compound, you think: Sies. If the alternative is a thousand descendants living on the premises, you think again.

We met a giant of a man in a tent town that the Weenen council had erected to house the unhoused. The giant proudly showed us round his kraal, which was well settled and spacious and evidently had tents for several wives and numerous children. 'Very nice,' I said, in the manner of one scrabbling for topics of conversation. 'How many children do you have?'

That question wasn't designed to pose a major intellectual challenge, but you would have thought it was the $64 000. He thought for a long time, and used his fingers, and finally pronounced: 'Fifteen.'

Then he immediately re-considered, said, 'No, wait,' and repeated the calculation, this time coming to the conclusion eleven.

But this didn't satisfy him either, and we started again. I was with the mayor of Weenen, the head of a minority tribe that believed in getting on with the Boere, to the disgust of some of the others. The dynamics became awkward, waiting for the giant to work out his children, and I was left complected.

On the one hand it was fairly painful to see the giant in this tent town situation, where he was sure that God intended him to have his own hill. On the other... the primitiveness, the irresponsibility, the lousy tragedy of this whole set-up was no fun at all. One of the 'solutions' was an initiative to settle a whole bunch of Zulu families on a 500 hectare farm about to be bought with public money. The mayor, a sweet enough guy, was in on this act. So was my old friend Graham McIntosh, former MP for the area. For their sakes, for the sakes of peace and hope and optimism, I'd love to say 'Great! Good! What a bright plan!' Unfortunately integrity obliges me to recognise that the sole real result will be the ruin of another 500 hectares.

Initially the Weenen farmers flatly refused to speak to us. They assumed that our business, as media, was obviously the business of showing them up as ogres. They had plenty of experience. Gradually one of the ringleaders, Peter Channing, chilled out. We visited his place in the hills — interminable miles of bumpy farm road, ending in the most spectacular view south of God's Window. Conversation consisted mainly of Channing pointing out scenes of murders and massacres.

I'd look down at the river far below and say, 'That's a beautiful river,' and Channing would say, 'Yes, and that bit that you're looking at is where five members of the X clan were massacred by the Y clan last Tuesday week.' I'd look around his stoep and say: 'This is a nice stoep,' and Channing would say: 'Yes, and those holes there are the bullet marks from when I was attacked on Boxing Day,' and so on.

We, South Africa 1996, continue to make this big thing of the Wild West of America, nineteenth century and distant and invested with a mantle of glamour and excitement while its reality was naturally the same pants-wetting banal brutality that warfare always is. We have a perfectly good Wild East all of our own, in full spate right now. In a hundred years there will presumably be the same kind of derring-do stories arising from the Natal of today as we have arising from the Montana of 1896, although whether the public version will be told from the Zulu side or the farmers' side is moot.

Channing showed us, in professorial detail, how he keeps his land in good shape: how he plants brushwood fences here, rotates crops there, detects incipient problems from analysing the colour and texture of soil, and so on. He took us to the border between his land and the Zulu land, and invited me to follow the fence way beyond its own visibility by looking at the line between the living land and the dead land. That line spoke louder than any quantity of rationalisations or sensitivities. This was real core Mother Earth we were talking about, not piffling Greeny superstitions about CFCs or nuclear power, and with my own eyeballs I could see earth alive and earth murdered. It's not patriotic to say in these circumstances: for the sake of equity let's kill off more.

Channing was the most unabashed landowner this side of the Amazon jungle. He said frankly and unconcerned that he protected his land with the gun, and that was that. I said: 'You know that sooner or later you are going to get shot,' and he shrugged. (He did get shot, six months later, and lived to fight on.) His frontier outlook is a world removed from the soft and trusting life I prefer to lead and where possible to cultivate, and I don't suppose we'd agree on anything from children's upbringing to women's roles to ethnic attitudes, but he left me with one profound revelation: the real land issue is not to do with title deeds or compensation or the manner of acquisition. It is about who sustains it and who starves it.

Later on the same trip we came across a newly ruined homestead. Here the Wild West metaphor was solid as concrete. We saw where the owner had been shot while putting finishing touches to an ambitious home-made irrigation system which had been systematically smashed. We walked through the pillaged house, stupefied by the extent to which absolutely everything other than the bricks had been looted. We saw the remnants of the ploughed fields, returning to jungle.

Nearly always, I'd come away from problem areas convinced that the problem was a lesser problem than met the eye. Coming away from Weenen, I had the opposite belief, and so I said. The wrap of the programme was a sad farewell on a hillside, a babbled garbled hurry while passing trucks disturbed the sound and the sinking sun disturbed the sight. In disoriented haste I tried to say: forget title deeds as the mainspring of redistribution, take the fallow where you can make it productive, but treat the productive as sacred.

This little spiel also touched the box's G-spot. It got across to places where I'd never get a planned and orderly written script to go. From whites, blacks, possessors, dispossessed, and all it keeps coming back to me: 'Gee, I never saw it like that.'

7
Land of Noddy

One of the more questionable joys of canned television is the institution known to the trade as the 'noddy'. The noddy is the device that enables editors to cut in to and out of sequences of conversation and is a necessary evil. I stress the word necessary. I also stress the word evil.

You're watching the box, right. Party A is talking about the price of eggs in China. Suddenly the camera cuts to Party B, nodding away attentively. At the same moment, lo! we're into a new sentence or a new point or a new topic. For a fleeting moment your ears have Party A's voice while your eyes have Party B's nods, and then — so smooth and so customary that you barely noticed it — you have Party A in sight again, still holding forth except now on the subject of the rock formations of Antarctica.

You've just met the noddy. Depending on how you choose to look at it, you have either been sandbagged by the noddy or saved by it. The editor has used it to abbreviate Party A's message to mankind, and by doing so he has either deprived you of the fullness of

Party A's wisdom in respect of Chinese eggs, or has protected you from being driven to sleep (or, worse, channel-switching) by lengthy boring minutiae.

In principle the same thing happens in all journalism. No writing journalist, even in purportedly verbatim Q-&-A interviews, ever prints literally everything his subject says by way of an answer. Nor, for that matter, everything he has asked by way of a question. For a start you naturally cut out all the ums and ers and repetitions. When you're inflicted with an interviewee addicted to 'in actual fact' or 'to tell the truth' or 'in other words' or any of the other extended versions of um and er, you cut those out too. That far, it's simple. From there on the tricky bits arise.

A degree of verbal diarrhoea is a universal condition of homo sapiens. Everybody says more in conversation than they intended to say. All that varies is the degree. In rare cases it is little, in many cases it is much. Normally you barely notice it, because normal conversation is built upon and lubricated by a natural overflow. Excess words are part of human interaction from start

Hullo how are you?
No fine thanks and you?
No lekker, and with you?
No use complaining, everything going all right hey?
No sharp and how's the family?

to finish

Okay so bye hey.
Ja see you.
Right drive safely hey.
Ja and look after yourself.
Okay, so long, don't do anything I wouldn't do.
Right, bye.
Ja, bye now.

Okay, bye.
Ja, bye.

All normal speech looks ridiculous in print. Conversely what would look forthright in print would sound offensively curt if anybody ever spoke that way. If someone addressed you in the words of a Time magazine interview, the apotheosis of pith and brevity, you'd want to klap him.

For print purposes you distil the essence of the human exchange. From a thousand-word conversation you might make a fifty-word story, and everybody is more or less happy. If you're my kind of journalist, uninterested in trapping people with slips, you give the guy the finished item in advance, and if he thinks you need a bit more of this, a bit less of that, he adjusts, and everybody's even happier, including the reader, who might think he is disaffected with the print media but is not nearly as disaffected as he would be if you printed interviews verbatim:

'We er sustain the level er because if we er do not sustain the level then the er level is um unsustained and when the level is unsustained then the plutohydrogenouschloride re-oxidises the latent ambient hypocinthal dioxide, like um er ah that time that er Doctor Smorgasbord was still um chief engineer, just before he moved to the er Putsonderwater branch or was it er first Hoenderhokfontein because of the um respiratory condition of his wife Petronella, and we learnt then that when the level er descends you know what I mean to below two thirds then there can be deleterious effects on Cape Town's water quality.'

Your genuine living and breathing comment for publication often sounds more like this than you think, prior to panel-beating. But as I said earlier in a different context there is nothing that can't be panel-beaten. There is no word in the dictionary beyond the reach of the print surgeon who can perform any amputation or transplant he wishes. As a print editor you are omnipotent. How you use your potency is another matter. You might quietly record 'Unless levels are maintained at two thirds the quality of Cape Town's water will be affected'. You might go in for the shock & horror bit: 'CAPE WATER POISON SCARE', probably accompanied by a tantalising strap such as *Apartheid Officials Implicated*. You can process it sensibly or you can process it otherwise, but you can process it to your heart's desire.

On TV, you can't pare it down to the words you want, because then it would be a series of short sharp jerks that look awful and smell fishy. You can pare but partially, and you pare with the noddy, an invention of the same value to TV editors as the horseshoe was to blacksmiths.

What happens with the noddy is:

I'm happily chatting with somebody — the mayor of Pofadder, the leader of a hijack gang, the premier of the Free State, the mother of a family murdered in the KwaZulu barbarism, whoever. We talk our talk, while Richard generates back trouble for his old age by swinging the camera from face to face, simultaneously manoeuvring to keep the light behind him and to keep the consequently intrusive boom shadow out of shot. Finally we're done, and the somebody is relieved to know it. Whereupon Richard says: 'Just stay there a moment, please,' and we're into noddies, and the poor interviewee is more bewildered than ever.

I sort of explain, but it's never that great an explanation. Aside from that we're usually meant to be 200 kilometres away an hour ago, I hate the noddies and am keen to get them over with as soon as possible like a visit to the dentist. Moreover, frequently the person I am talking to is going to remain bewildered whether I spend 30 seconds or 30 minutes explaining, so I tend to go for the short version, viz: 'Nowwejuststandhereforafewminutesandlookateachotherso-theeditorscanchangeshot, see.'

Whereupon the crew and I must reset the scene as it was. If there was a cow grazing all through the interview, that darn cow has to be sure to keep on grazing through the noddies. If there was a herdboy picking his nose, he'd better re-pick. Then the interviewee stands back in the place he was standing under firm instructions from Richard to 'just look at Denis'. So he looks at me, and it's a very weird experience to be 'just looking' at someone. You feel a natural temptation to *say* something. So he says something, and Richard, who is as conscious of the marching clock as I am although far more conscious of the editors' ire when noddies are short, says: 'Don't talk, just look.'

And while he just looks, Richard shoots him from front, from back, from top, from bottom, from right, from left, and inside out, and finally Richard shoots him from behind me; the 'over shoulder' noddie.

For the over-shoulder, my mouth must be moving. That's crucial, so we can slot this in to a place where I am asking a long-winded or lumpy question and thereby cut some of the excess out of the question. But of course for my mouth to be moving ought to mean there is sound coming out of it, or otherwise my companion will be seriously perplexed.

Anyway by this time my companion is thinking he has been suckered into some unwitting role in Funny People. So for about the first nine tenths of our shoots to date, what I would do is, I would say something reassuring. I would make some chatty friendly observation such as 'it's a strange procedure, isn't it, but you see it's necessary for the editing'. And when I said something comprehensible and communicable he would instantly feel a flood of relief, and of course would reply. Whereupon Richard, who could never understand why fate had cursed him with a presenter who screwed up noddy after noddy in programme after programme, would bark in distinctly terse tones: 'No talking please! Just look!'

I finally, recently, got beaten into the business of counting to ten or counting to twenty, which at least does not inspire my unfortunate interviewee to reply.

After he'd done his noddies, I had to do mine. Every now and again I'd scream and shout, metaphorically at least, and declare revolution, and refuse to take my noddies. This always made me feel like a child refusing to take his malaria pills. It would later make the editors back at Shaw Pictures feel like angels of vengeance.

They would take a grim delight, when they showed me the rough cut, in waiting for me to expostulate: 'This interview is far too long! We should cut it by two thirds!'

And they would smile through gritted teeth and say, slowly: 'We *know* that, Denis, but. there. are. no. noddies.'

In other words, they couldn't cut the boring bits out of the interview, because there was nowhere they could come out of a sequence and nowhere they could come back in to a subsequent sequence.

Abhorring the noddies with the passion I did gave me a fine incentive to invent alternatives. I kept thinking up all sorts of exotic variations, such as when we did a programme on art. I said: 'C'mon now, break a rule. We want to show a million artworks; we need a million noddies; so show an artwork every time you need a noddy.'

That was a slice of lateral thinking for you. If you'd looked at the results, which you didn't, because we delateralised the programme before it went out, you'd get a feel for why most developments involve good old linear thinking.

If the noddies failed to give me joy, their cousins the 'wides' were nearly as bad. A wide is a distant shot, showing the discussing parties from sufficiently far away that you can't see who's saying what, and it serves the same purpose.

Given that this purpose is standard journalistic stuff, why should it bother me? All journalism involves chopping people up. Let alone that the very basis of written reportage is to make concise what was not concise to start with, look at — er, that is, listen to — radio. Listen to the guys being quoted on the news. You can *hear* the commas at the ends of their excerpts. You know perfectly well that they were in mid stream, saying something that might have been profound or might have been stupid, you'll never know because the news editor arrogated unto himself the right to stop the tape at the comma. (For which, you are actually if subconsciously grateful, as you wish to spend only five minutes listening to the news.)

Moreover you see the noddy phenomenon virtually every time you watch TV. Even without the noddy, you also see, and take absolutely for granted, the related phenomenon by which all sorts of innocent people are endlessly portrayed as the authors of laughable and mockable one-liners.

This evening as I write the 8 o'clock news has just portrayed a suitably yuppie-looking American who is stranded in some place he does not wish to be because of the sudden revocation of Valujet's licence. How long this man spoke to the TV reporter I do not know. How many intelligent comments he may have made on the relationship between safety and daily routine, none of us will ever know because that footage, whatever it contains, was thrown out of the edit suite along with the empty beer cans. What was not thrown out was a sequence of about four seconds in which the character says 'I am very angry because now I have to spend a whole day here and there isn't even a hotel.'

Here is a neat bit of light relief. The American channel that filmed this clip was dedicated to the idea that Valujet is a danger to mankind. They had a heavy piece about how belatedly the FAA grounded the airline, and how slipshod the airline's checking processes were. But it was rather overheavy, so when their reporter happened upon a passenger whose life had been disrupted by the grounding, and when the passenger upped with his crisply mockable four-second aphorism, well, here was a cheap way to raise a giggle. Take his laughable four seconds, ditch all else he said, and let everybody − his third cousin in Nevada, his primary school benchmate in Albuquerque, total strangers anywhere from Louis Trichardt to Papua

New Guinea — sneer at him. 'Get a load of this idiot. His life has just been saved and he's complaining about hotels.'

This is standard TV fare, and by raising my worries about it I am by no means admitting that my show has a particular problem. Quite the opposite, in fact. The very raising of it indicates a degree of sensitivity to it, and a degree of sensitivity I certainly exercised. I went to comparatively extraordinary pains to ensure that my informants got a square deal. By 'comparatively' I mean 'compared to the average show I see when I push the Power button' and by this criterion 'comparative' is not automatically onerous.

But I tried. I tried. Put it on my epitaph! I tried to be decent! St Peter, are you listening? I tried!

Boy, and did I fail. I sometimes wake up at night, clammy and sweaty with the shivers about some poor innocent decent guy I'd done down. Even time, healer of all things, has difficulty with the clam and the sweat. What I'll *think* of, in waking hours, is generally the guy I did down yesterday or last week. What my sleeping mind, out of control, will *dream* of could be from any time, although more often than not it chooses to take itself back to August 16 1995 and that ostensibly innocuous subject, water.

I picked on water deliberately, and despite the good advice of all concerned. We'd had a batch of swing-on-ropes, leap-from-choppers, clamber-up-mountains programmes and I was fearful of becoming a kind of superannuated male answer to Melanie Walker, TV's action girl. We'd also had a pile of conflict-type shows, which inevitably harkened back to that standard South African story about the palefaces and the darkies.

As I saw it the Trek was meant to sustain at least some kind of intellectual element, oblique at minimum although by no means full frontal. Nor was the 'intellectual element' supposed to be one long round of The Blacks Think X and The Whites Think Y. So I chose water precisely for its unlikeliness and its potential for substance without racial split.

Water was at the time much in mind, mainly because of the general belief that we were about to run out of it. I thought it a challenge to take as unsexy a subject as water — water never wielded no guns nor knives, never bopped anybody on the head or shouted threats or spat hatred — and try to make it watchable (read 'entertaining') and a little bit thoughtful.

It sort of worked, although I didn't exactly escape the action-man bit. At one point I joined a bunch of Zulu villagers fetching water from a spring. I carried a bucket on my head back up the hill, and that sequence became the high point of the programme. I could understand that. It was hilarious, in the watching if not in the doing. I puffed up that interminable hill with water splatting and sloshing down my neck and drenching my clothes and irrigating the pathway, while teenage girls who came up to my ribs and weighed barely more than their buckets sashayed past me like speedboats running circles round an ancient crippled tanker. My back ached for weeks and for the first time I felt the meaning of the stories about regular water-carriers developing impacted necks and child-bearing difficulties.

As the programme unfolded it took an unintentionally scatalogical course. We connected with one Don Crawford from the University of Natal, who had designed a new brand of long-drop called the Phungaluthu, which means 'no smell'. Don's mission in life was to provide hygienic toiletry in places where waterborne sewerage is not an option, and he took it very seriously although not without certain wry acknowledgements of the humorous side of his trade.

When we met he said his job was abnormally privileged. He was the only person in the university who was paid to talk shit. Although I was normally puritan about four-letter words on the box, and bleeped out gratuitous swearing, this one in context was a sublime double-header, a whack at the arcanity of academe and a blow for the practicality of applied science, and I wanted it in.

Don didn't. We argued. We were standing in front of the Howick Falls, with sightseers coming, photographing, and peering quizzically at this weird conversation repeating itself over and again while Richard ran through tape by the kilometre.

I would say: 'Don, it's simple. I introduce you. I point out what you do, and then you simply say, just like you already did, "Yes, I'm the only person in the university who gets paid to..."'

Don would say: 'But it sounds coarse,' and I would cajole and blandish and twist arm and reassure. And Don would reluctantly agree and Richard would roll again and Louis would reposition the microphone boom to cater for the now altered position of the sun, and I would redo my little intro and would wait expectantly for Don's aside, and Don would draw breath... and there'd be a pause and the moment was gone and Richard would lower the camera and massage his aching shoulder, and we'd start again.

Finally Don baulked flatly, and there was nothing for it but that I had to say the dread phrase myself, as a casual parenthesis to my introduction. Fine. I'm supposed to be the pro. This should have been the work of a moment. Except that the crack had to be an extremely low-key aside, wholly deadpan, and I couldn't do it deadpan, particularly with a growing crowd of gawking tourists lined up beside Richard and cackling like the audience at a comedy act. It became like one of those schoolboy jokes where everybody knows the punchline off by heart and can barely contain themselves through the build-up before dissolving into hysterics at the crucial moment.

We got it more or less right at the end, but we'd set a new record. Normally the Trek is one-take shooting, noddies excluded. Sometimes it runs to two takes, occasionally annoyingly to three and very seldom much more than that. This time we had enough takes to fill a warehouse and I felt more sympathetic even than usual for the unfortunate editors back at Corlett Drive who were going to sit and roll their eyes through repeat after repeat of me saying the same thing.

What was worse, Don didn't learn his lesson. He had a wondrous facility for impromptu one-liners, which by virtue of our subject matter often involved an anal theme, and his natural wit was such that these things kept popping out and I kept wanting them on camera. Don remained coy, firming in his view that private wisecracks do not necessarily belong in public domain, and I accepted defeat in most of the ensuing fights.

But then, walking across a field while Don talked of the effects of inadequate sewerage, we came across a classic example of the effects of inadequate sewerage — a steaming human turd on the path. Don gestured to it, referring to it as a case in point, and went on with his hygiene lecture. Richard pulled the camera from us, zoomed in on the item in question, and returned to us in an unbroken movement. I interrupted Don and said to the camera:

'I sometimes wonder whether we bring you enough that is new on this Trek, and although this isn't quite the newness I had in mind at least it is the first time you ever saw a close-up turd on your screen.'

To which Don replied: 'Nonsense, there are close-up turds on the news regularly.'

And, wouldn't you know it, just as he spoke the tape ran out. So, of course, I wanted Don to do it again and, of course, he rebelled, and this one I wasn't giving up on, so we sparred and scrapped aanmekaar for hours. I didn't need Don's face on video, all I needed was his voice on audio, saying that same simple sentence in that same laconic way. Thus, escape from the locale was no escape and long after we'd left the scene of the crime I was still nagging.

In late afternoon we were in a forest at the Umgeni nature reserve, where Don had installed some yuppiefied versions of his long-drop for the use of eco-tourists about whose eco-oblivious defecatory habits he was very impolite. Don said: 'All

92

right, if you still want that sentence I'll say it, provided we shoot you making use of my Phungaluthu and you promise that this shot will feature.'

Well, now. We were already a long way deeper into toilet talk than I had ever expected or wanted to be, and this was pushing it way over the bottom. Then again I had been jabbering so hard about the turds on the screen that I couldn't chicken out, and on the following Tuesday the living rooms of the nation were graced by one of the less exposed portions of the human anatomy.

We did it with a certain discretion, I will claim. The rough cut dwelt on my posterior for numerous eternal seconds, using an awful device like an epidiascope's shadow to blur the focus. I blew dual fuses, at both the salacity of the length and the tweeness of the blurring, and we ended up with a — you will not believe it unless you saw it — tasteful picture of a guy taking a crap in the woods, as unblurred as the day he was born. It wasn't only tasteful, in fact. It was idyllically rustic in one of the more original, albeit earthy, ways yet discovered, not to mention a perfect ad for Don's loo.

Don's loo was thus an accomplice in the process by which I acquired the one and only national record to which I could lay claim, which is: The Most Overexposed Body in SA History. Between the Phungaluthu, and my endeavours to squeeze at 48 into a navy shirt I had been issued at 18, and being spied on through a cell keyhole while I donned prison attire, and being compressed into a rubber diving suit by several strong diamond divers who apparently thought they were rolling a carpet, and taking a compulsory shower upon entry to a mission for hoboes, and sundry similar experiences, not an inch of my undistinguished carcass has escaped infliction upon the camera's eye. Happily, the wastage rate for this category of footage set its own records. We did broadcast some part of each of these scenes, but with a degree of subtlety throughout.

About 99% of the tape in question was seen by no one but the editors, who at least got a laugh.

The water programme was a serious venture despite its excremental trappings. Don talked informatively on the design of the state-of-the-art long-drop, which has more to it than you would think. Aside from his smell-disposal techniques, there is the somewhat more basic factor that you must off-centre the pit, like this:

The way it has traditionally been done, world wide, is to mount the appurtenances directly over the pit, like this:

Which spells fantastically bad news for a few hundred South Africans each year; these usually being elderly ladies of substantial mass and little agility, whose weight the boards are unable to bear. For some reason the idea of a person falling into a pit of human waste elicits vast and common belly-laughs, but for those of us with upwards of two braincells to rub together it is not exactly a barrel of fun, especially not for the twenty per annum or thereabouts who end their days in the pit or their relatives who must dig them out.

I like the marvellously one-eyed comment from Jonathan Swift that 'he who causes two blades of grass to grow where but one grew before is of more value to mankind than all the race of politicians'. Strictly Swift is being sheer damfool as were it not for the race of politicians, with all their faults, there'd be jungle law and nobody causing any blades of grass to grow. But emotionally the sentiment is a terrific antidote to the smugness of the chattering classes, and if taken with suitable salt is an admirable one. People like Don belong with those who make two blades to grow. They get their heads down and their hands dirty and make poor lives better lives.

The same goes for Vincent Bath, the head of what everybody calls the Rand Water Board but now calls itself, streamlined and de-bureaucratised, sommer Rand Water, nineties-style. I knew Vincent of old from having kids in the same school and living in the same suburb (or nearly, he is officially in high-class Westcliff over the road from my middle-class Parkview) but had never known him well. We met him at Rand Water's head office in the glorious underrated hills south of Johannesburg, and I was half tempted to interview him in his rugbyfield office (which, like all New South African owners of grossly oversized public offices, he explained as bequeathed by the pretensions of the old era). But he persuaded us to head off to the Vaal river purifying plant and I'm glad we did.

We saw water rough and water smooth, water dirty and water clean, water in each step of the turn from the pea-soup colour for which the Vaal is named right up to the point where you'd be honoured to wash your false teeth in it, and I was honoured to meet the system.

This was real, this was respectworthy, this was stuff to make one proud. I loved encounters like this, the things that say 'hey, South Africa is strong and organised and working' and I revelled in slipping and sliding over the waterworks' mosaic of interleading dams with Vincent spelling the procedure out.

As usual the final cut embarrassed me in so far as Vincent's vivid explanations shrank to a scattered batch of viewer-friendly sound-bites. We somehow couldn't even incorporate his eye-opening revelation that the Vaal when it passes his plaas has shrunk to half the size it was when it got there, and we missed the punchy little debate that ensued when I put the proposition that South Africa should have no river deltas at all; that water flowing into the sea is wasted water and ideally we shouldn't complain, as we all do, about emaciated run-offs but should rather seek nil run-off, every drop to get dammed and siphoned and put to irrigation.

The naturalist in Vincent looked askance on this notion, but to me it becomes an ever realler option as the water squeeze tightens and I was sorry that the raising of it suffered from compression squeeze in the edit.

At least Vincent got part of his message across to viewers. He doubtless felt the standard regret, that he'd also said this and also said that and what the heck had happened to it, but his time was not wasted. Which is more than can be said for a good and decent water engineer at Sterkfontein, one Jan.

It'll be news to Jan, but he is the person on this planet who more than all others wracks me in penitence for the brutality of the goggle-box and my role as its henchman.

Jan took a day out of his life to escort me through the majesties of Sterkfontein, these majesties being exceptional.

Let alone the deep clean pure blue beauty, which leaves the shallow Gariep (née Verwoerd) looking like a mud puddle with elephantiasis, it is also the world's first dam to work upside down. It is not sourced by rivers following gravity from above in the fashion of the centuries, it is sourced by rivers being pumped upward from below, in a triumph of Seffrican vernuf and a model of sublime symmetry.

All day long Sterkfontein delivers power unto the masses, its mighty gates boosting the hydro-electric grid that gives Eskom more capacity than the rest of the continent put together. Come the small hours, when kettles are off and production lines are still, Sterkfontein uses its own lazy strength to pump the Tugela basin back upstairs into its own belly the better to mobilise the production lines again on the morrow.

Sterkfontein is the long-awaited perpetual-motion machine at last come to life, and if that isn't miraculous enough it also supplies its own excess H_2O to replenish the baths and showers and sprinkler systems of the Highveld. It had everything, this dam. It had technology writ large, it had exquisite landscape, and its dramatic outlet pipe − the grandaddy of all burst mains − was a guarantee of such sure-fire suicide that the sight, as we stood above the torrent, paralysed me with vertigo.

A jerky lift took us into the bowels of the machinery, where suspicious drips and leaks drummed awareness into mind and soul that many million tons of water hovered above your head. It could have been the setting for an epic tragedy of the 'Hotel' or 'Airport' genre, except that a problem here would hardly sustain two hours of cinema and a dashing last-minute rescue. To add to it all the place even had politics − if you think KwaZulu Natal is a bolshie province already, wait for the main act when its warring factions get their act together and start wondering aloud why Gauteng is swallowing their water.

Howcome, then, not a moment of Sterkfontein featured on the screen? Howcome Jan, when he watched the broadcast on that August night, had to rub his eyes in stupefied disbelief?

97

There was I, all right, invading his living room through the ether to restate the introduction that he had heard in lewende lywe while standing right beside me, and he had vanished. Where he had been, there was a symbolic portrait of a dripping tap. Jan was rubbed right out of the show. It was more insulting than mere disappearance; he had been downright superseded, and by a brass household faucet at that.

Many times I have been mortified by the disappearance of someone who has taken time and trouble for us. But on only two occasions have I collaborated in direct obliteration. Jan was the worst, being obliterated by a plumber's fitting. The other obliteree, Hennie, was at least obliterated by flesh and blood, albeit four-legged. Also, Hennie was the only aggrieved party who ever came back to tell me how it felt to fall off the screen.

I'm not telling you the circumstances of Hennie's non-appearance. In fact I'm not even telling you his right name. I don't think he'd appreciate it. What I do tell you is how I picture the night of the broadcast, building upon the skeleton which Hennie described to me.

Everybody knows this is Hennie's night. Hennie's gonna be onna teevee. And his one kid has ducked rugby practice, and the other has her boyfriend coming round, and Hennie's ma and pa in De Aar have phoned and said hey-hey, ou Hennie, we'll be watching, and Hennie's brother-in-law and his wife and their three are making a draai to watch together, and ou George and them from next door are dropping in to watch with Hennie and them, and the wife begins to feel like on wedding days and is in a frenzy in the kitchen and Hennie suddenly schemes there's not enough Castles, especially as ou Frans from the darts club rang to check he's playing tonight and Hennie said man no I'm gonna be onna teevee so ou Frans said s'true hey, okay I'll come sluk a lager with you and with ou Frans the lagers only touch sides after three quarts so Hennie does a rush to the bottle store and stocks a few quarts and then schemes no jeez man you don't want the okes to scheme you're tight so he stocks a few more quarts and then he schemes no jeez man you better lay on a bit of dop also so he stocks two bottles of Klipdrif and then he schemes no jeez man this is a like special occasion sort of and there is the ad right in front of him for the Fifth Avenue Cold Duck and the trolley is sagging but Hennie schemes man in for a penny in for a pound and some of these okes go in for a whiskey too, and now the living room is all crowded out and the peanuts and the chips and those sluglike orange sugary jobs are under pressure and Hennie's manning the bar and the wife's working up a sweat and ou Piet who dropped in and stayed when he heard Hennie's gonna be onna teevee is already ticking too fast for comfort, and then . . . Shhh! Shhh! and yes there it is, the programme just like advertised, and Hennie's saying ja, thassa oke, for sure, and the okes are saying where are you Hennie and Hennie is getting a funny feeling in his stomach and he's saying man I was right there nexta the oke, s'true'sbob, and the okes are saying so when do you come on ou Hennie, are they reserving you for the best or what, and ou Hennie is saying no well search me hey but I must be coming on soon I mean these okes spent the whole bleddy day cross-examining me, and . . .

And 28 minutes later Hennie has this skewered look on his face and the wife is smacking her fist on the table and saying you must bleddy sue them man you got your rights and the daughter is painting stiff upper lipstick over that let-down feeling and the son is thinking that he should of gone to rugby and dumb ol' pissed Piet is making raucous jokes about how the TV okes worried that if they put Hennie on the fillum it would break the sets.

And when Hennie got to bed that night he did not feel good.

If it's any help, me neither. Hennie was the only one who ever spelt out the sensation of feeling your moment on the nation's screen disappear as you watch, but there are plenty of other people who make me feel rotten.

There's Marcus Balintulo, rector of the University of Durban Westville, who sat with us until the shadows turned to night, explaining, discussing, philosophising – to have about a third of a minute passed on to anyone but me. There's Jan Mienie, colonel of the Mirage squadron, who spoke out firm and strong and honest on air force lore and airborne logistics and arranged a Mirage to play U-turns on a wet night's runways for Richard's camera to revel in the fireworks; and Colonel Mienie fell right off the screen.

There was Baleka Kgositsile, then ANC Chief Whip and now Minister of Ietsofanders, who allowed me to invade her diary and her parliamentary office and interrogate her on the urgent spot over the role of hereditary chiefs, and not a whisper of it saw the screen.

On the same Trek into chiefs there was the larger-than-life Mr Boltina, proprietor of the Savoy de la Boltina and scores of other Transkei enterprises. He was the most level-headed opportunist we met in Umtata and I hugely enjoyed the hour I spent in his incredible office and its leagues of velvet drapes with gold braid on every surface.

Boltina's hotel represented several firsts for me, such as the first time that as a paying customer I was required to park in the refuse pit, the first time that each of the bath taps, the hot and the cold, needed constant two-handed attention to make them run (so I ran the bath by alternate taps, a process requiring twenty minutes of undeviating concentration), and the first time that the switchboard, having listened in on a telephone conversation, happily rang back to say that the other party had misdirected me (this in several respects ranging from a character description of a local big-wig to the telephone number of KD Matanzima. 'And anyway,' said the switchboard, 'don't waste time trying to phone KD, the lines have been out for six months.').

The Savoy de la Boltina (the 'de la', said Mr B, is a 'nice cosmopolitan sound') is the kind of hotel that prompts one's local acquaintances to put a *big* curl on their lip and say, stretched out into five incredulous syllables, 'the Sa-a-vo-o-oy!? You're staying at the Sa-a-vo-o-oy!!!???'

It was a profound experience in Richard's life and has prompted him to observe, and restate approx 10 000 times at last count, that Beckett's Trek is perilous to health. His substantiation, aside from episodes like the flight from the refuse pit (into which we had been fiercely directed by a security guard), cites the insecurities that arose from his room, unlike mine, being affected by acrimonious negotiations between whores and their customers.

Me, I'd stay there again, at least in theory. (I've actually stayed twice in Umtata since, but each time with the entourage of a high priest of the new nation and therefore of course at the larniest hotel, the Holiday Inn.)

We'd got to the Savoy because I asked an excellent local character named Mkhululi Titi to make the arrangements. Mkhululi, a young and keen reporter at the Daily Dispatch and a non-passenger of the gravy train, did what he thought sensibly economical. He was mortified that the Transkei's gentry raised their eyebrows in united disapproval when the name Savoy was mentioned. He kept anxiously asking if he could change the booking to the Holiday Inn, which got Richard, Joe and Louis nodding eagerly. I vetoed it, initially on the principle that when in Xhosaland do as the Xhosa do. When the credibility of this line foundered against the evidence, I was still reluctant.

Partly, Mkhululi had tried so hard to do what was right. Partly... well, a Holiday Inn is a Holiday Inn is a Holiday Inn. It's like a Wimpy, clean and functional and short on soul.

It seemed to me that our business was the seeing, the touching, the hearing, the smelling and the feeling of Africa, and therefore we should do the seeing and the touching and etcetera wheresoever there was seeing to be seen and touching to be touched and etceteras to be etceteraed, not forgetting

101

even the smelling to be smelled such as there certainly was in the parking lot.

This is Africa's problem. The down sides are so often so visible, or olfactory, that the up sides get obscured. For the crew — NB, black Louis and black Joe not a whit less than white Richard — my sticking to this dump when at a snap we could have diverted to the portered halls of the Holiday Inn was a whimsy that exceeded the bounds of whimsicality and possibly even of eccentricity. For me it became a kind of statement, of belonging.

During the Savoy stay I at one point was waiting for service at the front desk. The duty receptionist didn't notice me. She was right next to the counter but turned away and distracted both by loud radio music and by a classy box of chocolates from which she was picking luxuriantly. I ahemed gently a couple of times with no effect and then said 'You must have a generous boyfriend.' She jerked erect with a smile to melt stone and in one smooth swift sweeping movement swung her arm up and popped a chocolate in my mouth before I had the chance to say Yes, No or Mmm, let alone refinements such as I'm Allergic or As Long As It's Not Ginger.

Whilst this response might not necessarily win top marks in your classical Customer Service training course, it struck me as possessing a certain charm, and at that a peculiarly African charm. You could look upon it as invasive, as unhygienic, as over-familiar, as a poor substitute for proper efficiency, as any number of wrong things. But you could also, if you choose, place a premium on it. I choose, and I regret that as yet this premium fails to blip the ratings. I believe that will change.

Once, on a flight in America, I had an especially excellent stewardess. She was so good and warm and companionable that at first I suspected some sort of competition was on the go, or maybe the airline's president was over the aisle. But by landing time she'd been sufficiently charming sufficiently long to dispel these churlish thoughts and replace them with an admiration for a way of life in which a stewardess could get such a belt out of doing her job so well and enjoying people so much and making so many friends.

Half an hour later I bumped into her at the airport bus rank and greeted her like the friend she had become. She looked at me as at a pushy stranger and turned away. It was like a splurt of repellent gas, and left me with an abiding sour memory. I'd been a friend while she was paid to be a friend, but it was a friendship she switched off like a light once it was no longer her job. I subsequently met several equivalent experiences of American customer service, exemplified by a cardboard plaque I stole from a hotel saying 'Our Guests Are Worth A Mint' and that is one reason I do not wish to live in America. I do not wish my humanity to be quantifiable like a brand of walking ATM.

The receptionist at the Savoy de la Boltina came from a different place in the human spectrum — human for humanity's sake. She pealed with laughter at the idea of a boyfriend giving her chocolates — 'Xhosa men don't do *that*' — and then attended with adequate aptitude to my needs. Whereas a corner of the mind may like to see the aptitudes of Africa become good where they are now adequate, not to mention adequate where they are now awful, there is another corner, and in my mind a big one, which prizes the chocolate lady and hopes the Customer Service smoothies will never panel-beat her into a walking talking substitute for the silicon chip.

She never made the screen and never expected to. Boltina didn't make it either although he did expect to. The airwaves remained virgin of the bit where amid Boltina's velvet I philosophised about efficiency and the allure of Africa. They remained equally, but more painfully, innocent of my cross-examination of a batch of Transkei hotshots as to why they automatically ran down the Xhosa-owned hotel and automatically extolled the whitest westernest least African alternative.

To which, I might say, the hotshots had damn poor replies —
something I was getting used to.

Precisely the same thing happened in Swaziland, where the
Swazi Business Council spent half an hour castigating my
heresies regarding affirmative action and five minutes later
were urgently advising me to stay anywhere other than the
Swazi Inn, it being no longer owned by Mr Cohen but now by
Mr Dlamini.

I don't say the Swazis were all wrong. I do detect flaws in a
hotel which can provide only voluble excuses when a guest asks
for eggs at breakfast. I don't say the Xhosas are all wrong
either, even though Mr Boltina's sheets were so well washed as
to quell concerns about the burn marks and the patches and the
rips. I do say that affirmative action gives many new meanings
to the notion 'bizarre'. It also creates a new notion of its own,
the African PhD, the Pull Him Down syndrome by which the
African middle class, that same middle class that is endlessly
shrieking 'appoint black execs!', immediately turns upon the
black exec you do appoint and shrieks 'Not him! That's the
wrong one! You're setting us up for failure!'

What was all wrong was the missing material. Especially
where it involved missing people. The Krugers, grandson and
great-grandson of President Paul, put their energies into
training performing seals in Schoemansville. Except their
second seal was mysteriously assassinated a year ago so now
it's 'performing seal', singular. I liked the seal, I liked the
Krugers, and the screen never saw them. There was the long
discussion with the angry Northern Province farmer who has
worked out proofs that the cloud-seeding people are causing
ruinous hailstorms. There was the nurse at Takalani Clinic who
gave us deep explanation about the particularities of psychiatric
work in Africa — 'they lock the child in an outhouse, he can see
nobody until he dies at twenty or thirty or forty years of age'.

There was Dorian Wharton-Hood, Deputy Chairman of
Liberty Life. I spoke to Dorian directly after coming from

1 *Four of the Trek's best features — Louis, Richard, camera, and an unlikely setting preferably of the kind that tingles your corpuscles with a sense of 'Ah! Yes! South Africa!' This one is in deepest depths of Kalahari, which is what I predicted would become the new name of North Cape. (The inconsiderate provincial government has failed to oblige, so far.)*

2 *The Free State's problem is: it's had a bad press. It is actually a place of class and culture aplenty, not to mention lots of lush green. Andy Grealey, a Free State boy from way back, revelled in shooting what ended up as a fairly lyrical Trek through that underrated province.*

3 *The day* before *the South African Miss Universe contest, Michelle McLean, a universal Miss Universe of a couple of years back, had been wearing short pants. She's 6 foot 1. That spells a lot of leg. For once the term 'stunning' was not a figure of speech. There were a lot of women managers among the staff preparing Caesar's Palace, which was handy as their male counterparts had difficulty concentrating. Our camera caught up with Michelle on the night of the award. She, and several other Ex Misses Something, demonstrated to my satisfaction that yes, this stuff* is *about personality as much as curvature.*

4 *In Cape Town, Patekile Holomisa is a common or garden Member of Parliament, with a tiny drab broom-cupboard office piled impossibly high with White Papers and Green Papers and Order Papers and Other Papers that he is supposed to read. (After journalists visit the habitats of MPs, they shut up about the 'gravy train' for several weeks.) This was no place for an interview. I said: 'Let's go to parliament's museum.' Patekile said: 'There's a museum here?' We got to the museum, a visual cornucopia of larger-than-life English kings in crowns and ermine and gilded frames and, with the smell of history thick around us, we fiercely fought over whether African chieftancy belonged in the late 20th century any more than English monarchy. My feeling was: to the dustbin with both these primitive institutions. Patekile demurred.*

5 *Later we called on his Great Place, half an hour or so from Umtata, where Patekile is lord and master of all he surveys and you gulp and think twice before getting flippant about chieftaincy.*

6 *It's not the weight, it's the manoeuvrability. Once you've got the thing balanced on your head it's fine apart from a certain bruising of the skull. Until you want to cross the road and need to check what's coming up behind.*

7   By the end, they were splitting their sides at my puffing panting reddened face. Plus that my bucket was more than half spilled out.

8   Major Nelis Genis was firm on certain aspects of aviation. Eg: (1) Flying *equals* Mirages and Impalas, and has nothing in common with freight haulage à la Boeings or boys' toys like choppers. (2) If I threw up, it would be my job to clean the cockpit afterwards. Nelis flung that machine through the sky like a psychedelic dream, with earth and sun tumbling and turning over each other second by second while my intestines alternately banged into my shoulder blades and bounced off my pelvis. I said at the end 'this has been a privilege' and I never spoke a truer word, even if I was at the time so green that for months viewers asked whether I had thrown up or not. (Not, but narrow.)

9   Never did I believe I'd feel deeply honoured to be flung in a mud puddle. An air force pilot gets the treatment before he sets foot on the ground after his first solo flight. Yes, technically I did take the controls to fly several million rands of State hardware over the Drakensberg at 500+ km per hour. Nope, relax, by no means solo. This was strictly honorary mud.

10 Colonel Nhlanhla Lucky Ngema came up with one of the nicer lines the Trek delivered. Behind him there was a huge prehistoric Trafalgar-type cannon, an incongruous sight in an air force base. I pointed at it and said: 'I see you're showing off your firepower.' He glanced over and, cool as you like, said: 'No, no, that's our new secret weapon, in development.' Ngema spent most of his adult life trying to wreck the air force he now proudly serves. Don't tell me the miracle was not miraculous; guys like him leave lumps in my throat.

11 Right here on this farm was where the Hon Derek Hanekom, Minister of Land Affairs and of Agriculture, was once arrested for High Treason. He was a touch surprised when I accused him of excessive pusillanimity re land reform.

12 Mme Megoe. 'Mme' does not mean 'Mesdames'. It's Tswana for 'Mrs' and it's pronounced with both Ms and a e as in bler. I love most of the people we meet on the Trek, but I loved her specially. She made me take home half a vanload of complimentary pomegranates, despite her insistence that white peoples are dedicated to ensuring that black peoples stay poor. She indeed had suddenly got rich, by a rip-off scheme that she was convinced came direct from The Lord Above. I saw a much sounder way for her and many other rural Africans to get rich, the only problem being: they're not going to do it. See Chapter 5.

13 *Mary Poppins' brother, obviously, in a field high above Magaliesburg, where the river rises. The field is protected by a fierce sign that misspells both 'trespassers' and 'prosecuted', so they couldn't expect us to know what it meant, could they now? We didn't often get into quite so outright a Rodgers & Hammerstein scene (I ought to be whistling the tune of 'Oklahoma') but wheresoever we found the sights and the vistas that evoke the things you love about South Africa, we'd grab 'em.*

14 *and* 15 *Orange Farm on a Sunday dawn. Sometimes, looking at the troubles and problems that the townships know too well, you can forget the other side: the elements of beauty and peace and honesty and effort, the people who out of little create much, in the way of cultivated gardens and immaculate homes and self-starting mini industries. Also, magnanimity of spirit, like the lady in picture 15 who, with the most charming smile known to mankind, told us how the family had been destitute since the death of their father several years ago but were making a go of it with herbal remedies.*

16 *Gathering of elders, Tugela Ferry, KwaZulu Natal. Minds failed to meet. I got ratty about their many excuses for failing to institute practical improvements such as contours.*

17 *At the Eldorado Park Fire Station they didn't have a pole to slide down when the alarm rings, and they didn't have a Dalmatian to run behind the fire engine. They had everything else, including long waits around the snooker table; false alarms that make you wonder how perverse perverse can be (and make the firemen feel ill with unfulfilled anticipation), and sudden rushes of incredible adrenalin. Also, sudden rushes of hurtling feet that left the blougat over here stumbling and bumbling his way into protective gear like Charlie Chaplin on an off day. This scene was shortly after midnight, on the way to a really horrible driving tragedy which a whole neighbourhood had seen coming up for hours. I'm wondering aloud when was the last time I spent an entire evening in stag company and nobody touched anything stronger than Nescafé.*

18 *What the heck is this picture doing in this book? It's providing a little relief from the publishers' insistence on the gross over-exposure of one particular face, that's what. This is a scene from a Trek. These are koi. There are thousands in this pool, and even the few you see are worth a tropical island holiday. This farmer figured that his traditional crops weren't delivering no more, in the changing economy, so he thought a little, and then made something else work. There's a lesson.*

19 There are times Africa can worry you. The fellow sitting with me on the harvester was giving me a thousand words about why he was unable to develop the patch of land he had nearby. Namely, because of the snake in the water source. Snake? Yep. A huge snake, bigger than the combi, which came out of the water with shining red and green lights.

20 Jeff Radebe, Minister of Public Works, showed me how his department was protecting rural KwaZulu water supplies from mud and cow-dung. It seemed to me they were spending a ton of public money on a function the people could perfectly well do themselves. When he finally got the difficulties through to me and I partly apologised, he reached out his hand with touching forgiveness.

4

5

18

20

crumbling tumbledown low-rent John Vorster Square, once a fortress that struck fear into many and death into some, now a run-down office building where windows are broken and linoleum is scuffed and there is no money for anything. By way of contrast Liberty Life's central atrium is a sci-fi Camelot, and I prevailed upon Dorian to come down there in order to tell me about businessmen's initiatives to combat crime. He spoke rivetingly and at length. He got about half a minute of screen time, which was at least better than Ken Owen, to whom we spoke on the same day re the same subject, crime.

Ken, by virtue of his pen and his cussedly individual mind more than his title as editor of the Sunday Times, was constitutional monarch of my profession. Not only that, he had some lovely lines. Right at the start I referred to the ultra-urban, New York-ish feel of his glass office in Diagonal street, and to the huge central illustration, the most radically anti-linear piece of modern art anybody ever saw. Ken commented matter-of-factly: 'That's my organogram.' You'd think we could have found him a comprehensible minute or two on the box.

Nope. His office disappeared and so did his organogram and nearly all his thoughts on the media role in fighting the crime wave.

When we looked into army integration we missed another organogram too – the painstakingly hand-made one which the black officers were crafting at a gigantic base in the Northern Province.

When I say 'gigantic', this base runs for over a hundred kilometres up the east side of the N1. Land redistribution? Speak to the army.

When I say 'black officers', thereby hangs a tale.

We pitched up late, as usual, and were nonetheless nicely received, as usual. Introductions proceeded as follows:

'Baie welkom, Mnr Beckett. Ek is Kolonel Van Staden en hier is Kolonel Van Schalkwyk and hier is Kolonel Van Deventer en hier is Majoor Van Niekerk and hier is Majoor Van

Jaarsveld and hier is Kaptein Van Huyssteen en hier is Kaptein Van Heerden...'

And it went on in this vein, and hands were shaken and greetings were greeted and all was terrifically amiable and harmonious.

And then I said: 'Eaoh, do excuse me but I don't believe I have met this officer.'

To which the response was: 'Um er oh ah er, yes, er, this is Colonel Msibi.'

And after Colonel Msibi we also came across Major Mbandla and Captain Msimang and a few more people who had been busying themselves in the background with what looked like a calligraphy lesson.

Which turned out to be not far from the truth. On the wall hung an organogram, a scrappy scrawled scratched-out and scrubbed-over bit of semi-legible board that made Ken Owen's artwork look almost geometric. Col Msibi & Co were doing a new one. Armed with crayons and koki pens, they were busy rewriting names and designations in a mock-gothic script which, Col Msibi assured me, was entirely his decision.

I got the firm feeling that Col Msibi didn't have all that much else to decide. He took me through the existing organogram, from which it appeared that he was second-in-command of the entire base and was also the commanding officer of a large section of his own, a section consisting mainly of Afrikaners. He and numerous Colonels Van Someone were quick to assure me that there is no apartheid in the army; no black platoons or white platoons; nothing like that. All brothers under the skin, getting along swimmingly.

Ja nee fine, except...

- No 1: While Msibi explained this, I could barely understand what he was saying. He was speaking in English, my home language, on a simple subject, and I found the combination of his accent, his grammar, and his vocabulary nearly impossible to piece together. I was now to believe that he

106

was in calm and confident command of a large body of people to whom he would also speak in English, not their home language, on everything from military discipline to guidance with family and personal problems? Pull the other leg.

- No 2: All day, I saw white officers giving orders, taking decisions, making things happen. All day, I saw black officers hanging around looking uncertain about their role in life.

- No 3: In the middle of this disorienting day, with everything I heard from the commanders being upbeat and gung-ho and everything I saw with my eyes speaking differently, a fire broke out. It started as a dinky ashtray-size fire when a sergeant flung a thunderflash for the benefit of Richard's camera. It was a small embarrassment, a thing that shouldn't have happened, which was maybe why nobody did any melodramatic smothering in the opening seconds, but walked over in dignified mien to stamp it out. Which was a mistake. By the end we had several scorched hectares and one pranged water-truck, and half the army unimpressively waiting around for someone to tell it what to do. I had the feeling that I and our production manager, Michael Modena, did more hand to hand fire-fighting than the soldiers did. In the course of all this, informality arose. I was no longer surrounded by men with pips and stripes, so the lowly troopies sidled up by the dozen to tell me about racism and bullying and sergeants calling them kaffer.

Now how do you get to the bottom of this stuff? Not with a camera, is for sure.

I will say that my programme on army integration incorporated a good many more cautionary notes than the norm. It also contained what must be the only suggestion anyone ever saw in public that the fault did not lie solely with the hangovers of the old regime but also had much to do with the gross over-ambition and under-application of the new crowd. But we didn't get to the nitty gritty. We didn't get properly to the virus.

You've been climbing your ladder for thirty years, you suddenly find someone magicked onto the rung above, the one you're reaching for. He's your son's age; he's a nice enough fellow, you get on fine except when you must report to him and seek decisions from him, decisions he can't make, on matters that you can handle painlessly. How do you feel?

You're thrust into an officers' mess. Everybody is terrifically nice to you, and makes every decision in your absence. You're estranged from your old comrades, who must now salute you and call you Sir. With your new comrades you have only small-talk. You know they're inwardly humouring you; they don't believe you can handle the command you're supposed to be in. Sometimes you think they're right, at least in terms of their systematic rule-bound traditions. You read the paper all day, you don't know what else to do. How do you feel?

I ended the army programme grumpy towards all concerned and dissatisfied with the value of what we'd done. I at least enjoyed a service-rivalry joke that one of the soldiers had told me and I delivered this as the closing note. It went:

Mandela one day wonders how his security forces are shaping up, and decides to run an impromptu test. He phones the chief of the army and the chief of police and says to each: I'd like you to bring me a crocodile before nightfall.

So the chief of the army calls his strategy men and his tactics men and his infantry battalions and transport battalions and all, and they draw up campaign plans and operational codes and then they go out and do it, and at nightfall they deliver Mandela a crocodile, neatly bound and trussed.

Meantime the chief of police has ordered: get the president a crocodile. The police jump in their yellow bakkies and drive around like stockcars, burning up rubber and petrol and pedestrians' nerves. Mid afternoon they meet in the kroeg to discuss progress. Discovering there isn't any progress they have a drink or two. Suddenly the commissioner discovers it's almost nightfall. He yells at Internal Stability: hey, hardloop, go find a likkewaan, beat it till it confesses it's a crocodile, give it to the president.

Colonel Msibi was one of many soldiers who did not feature on the airwaves. A pity, visually, as he is a great strapping giant of a man; central casting's perfect military officer.

Then there was Superintendent Frik Kitching of the Fraud Squad explaining why it's a lot easier to catch the two-bit crooks than the big-timers. There was the committee of the North West Provincial School Sports Association, a fascinating cultural exchange over when and where non-payment of fees should be tolerated, with everybody playing to the camera like troupers. There was the air force recruits intake who marched until their boot leather was wearing out while the camera studied them from every possible angle. There were the *lady* airmen whom I begged and pleaded to say something more meaningful than 'fine' and who finally came up with a cry of rage about their male peers.

There were too many to record. I believe that every vocation has a drawback. Mine has only one that seriously bothers me: the hurt I render to people who fall off the screen.

I apologise. I apologise belatedly to all I have let down. I apologise in advance to all I will let down yet.

8
Rave On

Which were the best, which the worst? The question is easy and I am asked it daily. The answer is hard, and changes from one asking to the next.

The Treks I like are those where we struck a balance between the fun factor and the enquiry element. The Treks that keep coming up in people's comments are not necessarily the same. Three in particular come up all the time: hijackers, taxi wars, Raves. Two slices of brutal savagery, one slice of yuppie fun. Sounds like a sandwich recipe. Is it some kind of metaphor?

The Rave was the easiest programme we ever made. It was also the one I was most reluctant to do.

When Keith first said 'Let's go to a Rave' I said 'A what?' This was in November '95. Keith felt that turmoil in the townships and barbarism in KwaZulu was fine and well (as subject matter, that is) but that we had more suburban teenyboppers in our audience than kraalburners in Ingwavuma; what about something for and about them? What about young people's nightlife? Moreover, he said,

nodding dutifully to the sensitivities of the New SA, we can incorporate youth all round. We go to a Rave, where the white kids go. Then we go to whatever the black kids are going to. With me this flew like a brick balloon. I'd only dimly heard of the Rave, which I gathered from my kids and their friends revolved round (i) drugs and (ii) a frantic hammering beat composed by computer, untouched by human hand. And a previous attempt to figure out what black kids do by night had delivered a short answer: viz, that the townships die at night. From about 9 o'clock onwards the roads are empty and you're lucky to find the occasional drunk staggering home from a shebeen; shebeens themselves being impossible places to film because everybody but the mama is out of their skulls, and there is so much racket that you have no idea whether the mama is saying 'Do have a Castle' or 'Go home Whitey'. Furthermore I was anti the whole image of a kiddies programme, and my chilly response froze the idea over.

But then came April '96. We were hopelessly behind schedule – doing everything at the last minute, never a programme in the can in case I caught a cold or broke a bone – and it was beginning to look as if Keith had been ahead of his time. The Rave was becoming a fat talking point, and my kids' erstwhile snotty attitude had modified into an envious quizzicism.

One pressurised night we dropped plans to ogle the up-and-coming KleinKarrooFees – too far, too prolonged, and time was out – and while searching for a speedy substitute Keith said an ultra-rave was coming up, billed as the Mother of All Raves.

So at 10 pm Friday night I pulled up at what I knew as Shareworld. I felt like a cross between Rip van Winkle and the Ancient Mariner, being the only person in sight older than 30 and a long way older to boot. What I must have *looked* like is a cross between sugar-daddy and dirty old man, driving up in your classic menopausal 12-cylinder red sports car with two pretty teenagers as my passengers. In fact this was deceptive. The girls were my daughter Meave and her friend Theresa, and the car was the same age as they were (and whatever the truth of the psycho-pop penile theories about the possession of exotic vehicles, I'd been driving Jaguars for 30 years so at least it wasn't a mid-life thing).

The crew was on hand. We rolled two cameras with barely a let-up, and went home with the eastern sky lightening. A doddle. If I could compress every shoot into a short sweet single eight-hour burst this would be my 19th book and not my 3rd.

This Rave was nice. Some things about it were remarkably nice. One of these was expressed with earthy accuracy by Michael Modena: 'You know,' he said, 'there's none of that tell-tale smell of vomit behind the tree.' Another was the mood around the place, which I summed up in the observation that when you stood on someone's toe he did not hit you, kick you, knee you, or stick a knife in your ribs; he said 'excuse me, you're standing on my toe'. Whereupon you said 'oh, sorry', and he said 'not to worry', and it was about as civil as civil can be. Then, to the best of my knowledge nobody driving home wrapped his car round a lamppost. Whatever the contentious rave drug Ecstasy does or does not do to you, it is common cause that it at least does not leave you seeing skew like trusty traditional alcohol.

There were between 10 000 and 20 000 people at that place that night, I don't know if anybody had any particular interest − tax-wise and so forth − in keeping the figures too very meticulous. Either way this was one large crowd, and I had never known a night so long with sound so loud and a crowd so large pass with zero aggro.

This night did. At about 4 in the morning I hunted down the paramedical station, where the ambulance guys were playing cards. I asked what action they'd seen and they said that every half-hour or so they had to deal with a dehydration case. I

112

didn't see a fight all night; an otherworldly experience in relation to my own memories of juvenile jolls meaning keeping constant guard for the spoilers and the weight-throwers and the muscle-bound bastards who wanted to choon your chick.

The sole discordant note at the Rave was a grumpy character who flung a huffy when Richard courteously asked him if he'd relinquish a certain vantage point for a moment. This fellow grouched loudly about TV people thinking they had preferential privileges, and although he could have grouched less obnoxiously I couldn't object to his central point.

In another respect, for which Rave culture bore nil blame, I suffered from major heebie-jeebies. I was probably the only one among those thousands either old enough or interested enough to have known that this same venue had been the scene of a tragedy.

A decade ago, when Shareworld was still all bushy-tailed about the coming-together of the nation and was meant to be the focal point of the new harmony − vide its name, and its symbolic location halfway between Johannesburg and Soweto − there had been a fire in its cavernous bowels, and there were young people inside, and the exits were blocked, and limbs were broken and chests were crushed and there were corpses. How many corpses? I do not remember. What I remember is feeling that if this had been Britain or America the name Shareworld would have become an international simile in the manner of Hillsborough. Being where it was, the event was not even a nine-day wonder. Three-day, maybe. I also remember that all the kids were black, which went a long way to explaining the three days. If they'd been shot by policemen they'd have been biographed and eulogised and would feature in scrolls of honour. Being tromped by their peers they were another grain in the desert of African woe.

They were also a poignant posthumous judgement on the sharing of Shareworld, a gigantic Disneyish stucco monument to the failure of good intentions.

My friend Bobby Godsell won't mind if I paraphrase a lesson he put in my mind. Shareworld and Sun City appeared at about the same time. They took different routes. If Sol arrived at Sun City and found an unpolished doorknob, somebody was out of a job. At Shareworld, if there was no hamburger at the hamburger stand, no cooldrink in the cooldrink stand, and no tickets at the turnstiles, the management would say 'sorry about that, but do understand that we are supporting emergent business'.

One result is that Sol's empire went global and provides more employment every year, and Shareworld went down the tubes taking R34 million of Standard Bank's conscience money with it. Another result was goodbye to the sharing. Instead, Shareworld became yet another milestone on the long route to an entrenched perception that when the blacks move in the facilities cease to work.

True, it was probably wishful thinking in any case to hope that your white kids from the north end of the highway and your black kids from the south end would meet in the middle and exuberate in bonds of amity. There was fright and there was fear and already the whiteys were on the run from the advance guard of the black incursion, even if in those days the run was a trot compared to the current headlong hurtle. So Shareworld's wicket was a touch sticky from the start, but the decline was massively accelerated by the utter morass that passed for management.

I was there a few times, mainly for functions of a nature that was not yet jargonised as 'politically correct'; sometimes as an individual putting my tuppeny's worth into the sharing ideal. Once, at the launch of the Sowetan's Nation-Building campaign, I spent some 70 minutes as part of a vast crush of penguin-suited males trying to find liquid for themselves and for the ladies they'd left in the adjoining hall to make forced conversation in ballroom gowns. Every time every barman was asked for a mixer or a cooldrink, he would take a 2-litre bottle from a cupboard, unscrew the cap, pour, rescrew the cap, and return the bottle to the cupboard. Next customer: 'Coke, please', same procedure. A supervisor, looking studiously superior, lounged in the rear carefully avoiding catching anyone's eye and carefully avoiding doing any actual work.

It wasn't just pathetic, it was surreal. You couldn't quite escape the suspicion that somebody was taking the mick. No real business could be as direly inept as this. The penguin suits didn't know what to say. Half the bodies inside the black-and-white uniform were so-called black bodies (more accurately brown) and half were white bodies (actually pink) and it was a time that nobody could say what everybody was thinking, viz: 'This service is so bloody awful that this company should be put out of its misery.' That would be racist if a white mouth said it and treason if a black one did. So the alleged cream of Joburg society, crammed shoulder to shoulder and eyeball to chin, passed the time in plastic smiles and strained small-talk while the more enterprising of their parched womenfolk next door drank water in cupped hands from the cloakroom tap.

Places like that, you don't go back, and the emergent business ceases to emerge. When the whites don't go back the dis-emergent businessmen say, 'See, it's racism that did us in.' When the blacks don't go back the businessmen say, 'These people have no loyalty.' The ineptitude is exceeded solely by the hypocrisy.

The Rave was Shareworld's short-lived phoenix. Shareworld being the biggest indoor venue around, presumably the biggest in the country and the continent, the Rave organisers got it dusted off. It was 10 years since the last time I'd been there, and I was sorrowed to be reminded of the ideals it had originally represented: the we shall overcome and hand in hand and black and white together etc. This time it was 3 in the morning before I saw a black African face. It belonged to an employee bringing a crate to a drinks counter, on her head.

To be reminded of the fire and the stampede of that previous era, I was alarmed. Human goodwill was fine but sardine packaging was not. There were periods and places where it was impossible to move at all; others where snaking queues inched at snail's pace between the thunderous dancing of the centre and the cool air of the periphery. I had told Meave and Theresa to meet me at the door at hourly intervals. Strictly, this was good old pointless paternal paranoia, and would have been nil help if a fire broke out at a quarter past the hour, but there was a certain reassurance in the hourly evidence that they had not yet been overtaken by the terrible fates that were direly predicted, such as being assaulted, abducted, enslaved, or endrugged.

Which was where the trouble came up: drugs, and specifically that at the end of the programme I said, in effect: 'I'm a less worried parent than I used to be, Rave-wise. It's a pity that a drug mentality lurks close beneath the surface, but I can't see that anybody's getting forced into drugs and moreover I'm not persuaded that all drugs are always disaster.'

Well, wow. Timothy Leary rides again. Dedicated anti-druggies were infuriated. I had parents — I still do — saying things like 'we hear you're encouraging our kids to take drugs'. I had angry letters and worried letters and frequent copies of the same light-weight little wire-service article that had just featured in several newspapers, saying that Ecstasy was suspected of having caused 10 deaths in the last year.

Nobody became abusive (demonstrating once again that the South African public has more civility than its individual members like to credit it with) but many were cross. Had I done a disservice? I've had plenty of time to reconsider and I've never been scared to recant. This time, I don't recant.

On the night I didn't get a proper take on the drug prevalence. Plenty of people confidently asserted: '*Everybody's* stoned, you're the only one who isn't.' Plenty of others said: 'Not us, we don't touch the stuff.' Some of these were doubtless pulling wool over a geriatric pair of prying eyes. It was difficult to know who to believe, but I believe Meave, and on that I place importance.

A while earlier there had been a Saturday night murder at the White Horse Inn. My 702 show on the Monday night was full of unusually youthful callers, whose main message had been 'Of course we don't tell our parents what we're up to. They say No No No all the time, so we deceive them. We tell them we're staying over with friends to watch TV.'

I know that my children don't deceive me. I don't want them to ever begin. For that reason not least I am careful about the No No No line. I hope they never set foot on any mind-buggering avenues whatsoever, preferably including the alcohol avenue that their elders treat as a commonplace feature of adult life. But I am alive to the social pressures and the attraction of the easy escape and the excitements of the unknown, and therefore I do not care to say: 'My kids are above it.' I prefer to seek to ensure that if ever they were to find themselves in a tangle on this matter, they would keep their parents informed and rely on our support.

To achieve this purpose, it seems to me necessary to apply flexibility. We, today's adults, tend to have a straightforward idea that drugs = bad news; gutters and crime and despair and human devastation. But, as has become the ultimate cliché of modern times, this is nothing if not a changing world, and up front among the changes is new and diverse chemical discovery, behind which psychological and medical understanding trails at an enlarging gap.

The exciting unknown gets more unknown by the day. Somewhere between tobacco and cocaine, somewhere between beer and heroin, there is a mushrooming range of newfangled ingestives that oil the cogs of the brain in a million uncertain ways. For all I know – and, I submit, for all anyone knows, scientists and psychs and chemists and all – inside that range there lie substances whose plus effect upon overall human welfare is massively greater than their minus effect.

Already wonderdrug Prozac, as legal as antibiotic, has given apparently harmless happiness to hundreds of thousands of previously miserable people. How does Prozac, medicinal and thus kosher, differ in impact upon mind or morals from Ecstasy, recreational and thus taboo? Search me. With respect you can just as well search Mr Upright Uptight pounding the dinner table so the pinotage rattles while he expostulates on the downfall of the modern generation. And for that matter you might as well search The Economist, the world's most authoritative magazine, which also can't figure out what's wrong with Ecstasy other than that its dehydration effects might kill 1 in about 3,5 million users. If that's the criterion for banability, the drug comes a long way below cars, pools, horses, or fun-fairs.

It's not that I want kids using it, but that if they're going to use anything rather let them use the relatively benign. At the Rave there was no real Ecstasy on display. There was a kind of gungy jelly called by the lucratively disgusting name 'Toxic Sludge'. It supposedly contained rum or brandy, but the one I bought made me suspect that the chef had been conserving his spirit supplies. A cooldrink called Guarana was supposed to contain exotic South American herbs that the purveyors say gives energy and the critics say blows minds. Mine might as well have been a Fanta except its 340 ml can cost R6 where Fanta weighs in at R2. And come to think of it, haven't they been sneaking some suspicious secret ingredient into Coke since 1865?

I don't want my kids to feel a need to get into mind-messing. But I don't believe it will stop them to invent horror-stories that do not always exist. It is undisputable that drugs have wrecked lives. It is eminently disputable that the answer is a fanatical blanket No as favoured by many within the drug-fighting field. I'm not apologising for what I said, and I remain confident of

Meave's assessment, which is that of the friends she met there some were flirting with liquor, some were flirting with Ecstasy, a heck of a lot were saying 'my mind is fine as it is, and I can have a good time without bending it', and nobody was trying to inveigle her into the drug world.

For the Trek team in our role as purveyors of public entertainment, the reaction to the Rave was instructive. Keith had been right. We deal with a yuppie issue, and we get comments, queries, wisecracks, criticisms and all-round feedback in a tidal wave that completely overwhelms the norm.

The norm, it should be said, is not vast. In my experience the norm is never vast. Whether you're talking newspaper, radio or TV, nobody who engages the public via public media ever gets reciprocally engaged to anything like the extent he thinks he ought to be. Casual comments, yes, there's a perennial flow of 'nice column' and 'liked your last programme', although this need not necessarily mean that the commenters actually read your column, or anything. Much of it is plain courtesy, the media practitioner's variant of the sentiment that to other people would be expressed as 'you're looking well', or 'nice tie'. I'm by now accustomed to hearing a regular supply of 'never miss your show' or 'your column is the only thing I read', months or sometimes years after the show or column concerned has come to an end.

I've known media people get sniffy about receiving false congratulations, and I have a dim memory of having in some previous aeon manifested a sniffiness of my own. I have long since graduated, thank heaven, to the only worthwhile way of handling a life involving public activity, which is to assume unless and until proved otherwise that nobody you meet knows who you are, ever saw or read or heard anything you did, or cares a continental curse.

Casual comments aside, if you get five actual considered letters in response to a particular appearance, that's a lot. If you get 10, that's a freak, and more than 10 is a mystery. The Rave

— the most talked-about episode of a well-rated programme on a public TV channel — must have delivered about 30, which is far lower than the number of times I have been orally required to talk about it.

There's perspective for you, although I'm not sure what the perspective proves. Furthermore while those 30 letters, all denunciatory, constitute the second highest individual mailbag I ever had, they come an extraordinarily poor second to the No 1, which, not at all denunciatory, derived from an article of which a mere 10 000 copies were printed, in Frontline. It was a 13 000 word — ie the size of a young book — account of my car breaking down in the Karoo. When after 6 months or so I abandoned the intention to reply individually and resorted to the photocopier there were 266 letters in the file. About a hundred more followed later. A bit of finger maths thus suggests that in so far as purposeful response is an indicator of consumption quality, a small publication might deliver a hit rate of 1:30 where a large TV channel does 1:300 000.

How do you explain this? Don't ask me; all I know is that media planners of the 21st century are going to look closely at such issues. Why am I mentioning it? To brag? Probably, but my hidden agenda is that I am again the publisher of a small magazine, and my excuse is to show the exception that proves the rule.

The rule is that media interaction is one way traffic. The most common number of deliberate responses to any media input is nil. When you see, as you periodically do, periodical columnists writing things like 'thanks for your hundreds of letters and faxes', what you're seeing is a new columnist whom you can reasonably bet is not going to become an old one. If five people in this great nation and wide take the time and trouble to put finger to keyboard in reply to something you have said, be honoured. Also, be slightly beset. Five letters sounds piffling but means five replies requiring you to put finger to your own keyboard, or, if you're organised, to the button of dictaphone, which is only marginally less time consuming.

So be grateful then for the shopping-mall compliment, which holds out less interpretability but also requires less surrejoinder, and is where the Rave delivers its lesson. The Rave is four months old as I write, but it hasn't even started to fade. For every one person who says 'I saw you carrying water on your head', or 'I saw you flying that air force jet', or 'I saw you being put into prison', or all the sights of the other 45 Treks collectively, there are two or five who say 'I saw you at the Rave.'

At face value there is a simple lesson in here: produce material that affects a white urban English market.

Unfortunately this is not a lesson I wish to hear. For me the challenge, the excitement, the wealth, the health of South Africa all lie in breadth. It's a world in one country, like Satour says, and I want it all. I want to throw jukskei with the Boere in the Marico. I like sitting on a diamond trawler's deck discussing philosophy with a bunch of coloured divers while my feet unfreeze after a trip to the Atlantic seabed. I want to hear the religious Indians at the University of Durban Westville talking about their upset that the new African-dominated SRC allows liquor on campus. I enjoy meeting the old aristocracy of Alexandra township and getting a glimmering of their rows with the cheeky newcomers who think they're equal. I find it fascinating to sit on a hilltop in the middle of a panoramic valley the size of Belgium while the Inkathas tell me why it is their moral duty to bulala the ANCs and the ANCs tell me the opposite. The last thing I intend to do with the Trek is turn it into an insular little commentary on the comings and goings of the charmed Wasp triangle that fans north from Braamfontein between D F Malan and Louis Botha avenues.

How were we to reconcile an eclectic bias like this with the focused message that experience delivered? Not well, but there were helpful features. For one, it slowly became apparent that the roar of Rave-talk was a roar we were indeed hearing in the malls: in Cresta, in Hyde Park, in the Firs, in the Square, in Northgate — in the little batch of parallel retail precincts, all inside the charmed triangle, which tap about 40% of the nation's disposable income. This was where practically everybody connected with the Trek lives.

If we'd lived in Qusililulu or Vendusiespruit or Hluvamaduba or Jakkalsfonteinkop or Shisakhashanghondo or Telemachusspruit or Kobonqaba or Sheridan or Darglestream or Tshamavhudzi or Hlahlalefsielo or Victoria Gulley or Chuhwhinipan or Sekghophokgophong or Dassiekranskop or Kilmarnock or Spekrivierskloof or Committeesdrift or Diphudubhudu or Visagiesfontein or Spoegrivierbaai or Xuxuxa or Percydale or Zwavhumbwa or Potloodspruit or Umhlambanyati or Horse Tail or Ibhobhobho, whose retail precincts jointly tap perhaps 0,00000000001% of the nation's disposable income, we might just hear a different sound.

Which is the point. What are we doing on that box? Are we there for the delectation of the yuppies and the boorjoes, or are we meant to have something to do with the growth and maturing and unifying of the larger nation? I know what my answer is. I don't suppose it's necessarily the same as the answer the SABC's marketing ouens would offer, but then they don't bother me so I won't bother them. For me, the name of the game is to paint across as broad a canvas as I can physically traverse, season for season, until some unpredictable day some suit-wearing title-bearing personage rings a bell and says 'Right, next act please.'

Among business-minded enquirers, my feelings on this matter tend to cause something between disdainful sneers and cardiac arrests.

'Tell us,' they say, 'in what way does the market drive your show?'

'In no way whatsoever,' I say, 'and long may that persist.'

Which is heresy. The commercial buzzword of our times is 'market-driven'. Every seller of a service is supposed to be constantly cupping an ear to what his market is telling him it wants. That may be fine for a toothpaste manufacturer, although he too will of course have ditched the Market-Drive fad in a year or two like he ditched the Excellence fad before it and the Objectives fad before that and the Opportunity-analysis fad before that and all the management fads that have turn for turn been the rage of their day.

But it is no use to me. Even if I accepted that our audience was the A/B-income elite, which I do not, it would still be no use. I know perfectly well what they would say if we asked them what they wanted. *Excuse me, sir, would you prefer a programme about property prices in upper-class residential areas or a programme about public works efforts in rural KwaZulu?* It doesn't take Sherlock Holmes to detect the answer. A 'market-driven' programme would be a prison. Better to take the approach of indulging your instinct (which, incidentally, I will take good odds on becoming the next management fad or maybe the one after) and setting out to make it sufficiently absorbing to take your market with you.

So far, touch wood, the Trek record re the indulgence of instinct has been fine — a dashed lot finer than I have managed with my two magazines (which is largely because of the radical difference in scale). Much of the reason that the upper-class establishment would turn up its nose at a survey question about the public works of KwaZulu is the expectation that this would mean a stolid diet of shame and guilt. We have tried to leaven the Trek with a modicum of the unexpected, and as far as we or the SABC can make out the result is that we are certainly not suffering in the A/B zones, whilst apparently picking up a reasonable audience in the nation's other corners as well.

Currently two streams of thought reside in uneasy coexistence within the corridors of broadcasting power. The overall philosophy is to celebrate the rainbow nation. The hard-headed budget-drawers charged with bringing in the income would prefer to segment their channels and offer the advertising world a neat demographic audience profile. In the end the forces of finance will doubtless prevail, in that compelling way they have, and in the meantime we're not oblivious to them. We aim to deal with the broader nation and as long as there is a Beckett in the Trek so we will continue, but to deal with it in a way that speaks to the Sandton surgeon, or the Paternoster fisherman or the Reservoir Hills priest, even while the subject matter is the Sekhukhuneland peasant, and as far as possible, vice versa.

There are plenty of rewards attached to the Trek, but few match the experience of having somebody utterly unlikely — it could be an Afrikaans railway artisan in Welkom, it could be a Zulu schoolmarm in Nqutu, it could be a Pedi schoolkid in Marble Hall — accosting me to say that something we've done has added to their faith or their hope or their understanding.

Not often do those people refer to the Rave.

9
Close to Crime

The Rave scored big in the charmed triangle. Two other Treks scored across all social corners, from Sandhurst to Sannie-shof, Aasvoëlkrans to Zwelitsha. They were both about crime. I'm sick of them.

Each had a high-point scene, both of which have now featured in several repeats and promo clips. Both times the camera only caught a portion of the reality. In the one we see me gormlessly wondering why some-body's playing firecrackers in the middle of the day while in the background sergeant Deon Esterhuizen, declining to hang around and elucidate the ignorant, cocks his rifle and starts running. In its own right it's actually a pretty good scene, although it does not reflect the full panorama that struck the naked eye when five thousand people tumbled and rolled and fell down the hill on the west side of Johannesburg's Bree-Sauer taxi rank and one (1) single individual charged the other way.

This individual was Deon. He was run-ning into a sudden and unforewarned taxi war. As he got to the top of the hill, a

solitary youthful bantamweight in blue uniform, the war stopped. He stopped it, simply by the application of insane courage. As he arrived, voices yelled 'Poyisa! Poyisa!', damn surprised at the speed with which 'the police' had pitched up and unaware that 'the police' consisted of Deon alone, and the assailants split in a hurry.

The camera saw the gist, all right, but the bit that stays clearest in my mind is the Black Sea parting as this isolated sergeant scythed through it to put his life on the line. The episode made me shorter of shrift than previously with the oft-repeated line about 'you whites consider black lives cheap'. As it was there were several black lives snuffed out, not by white hands, at the taxi rank. There would have been a hang of a lot more if Deon had chosen the route of taking cover and radioing for reinforcements.

That scene has been replayed often enough for plenty of people to be sick of it by now, but only one is sicker than me, and that is Deon. He's sick of me writing about it too. All he was doing was what he was there to do, and he's half embarrassed by the medal they gave him on the strength of my evidence. He's a fourth generation policeman, and at least his grandad is proud as punch over the unwont recognition. Deon was shot the next week, hit in the hand, which I gather may not work properly again.

The big hit in the other programme was where we call on a gang of hijackers in Soweto (which incidentally was not much harder than calling on a hotel; we asked a couple of people and one offered to take us). The scene has a gunman shrieking and threatening as he pulls his brother out of the driver's seat of my car. I've seen it enough times for one life.

In this one, the bit the camera only half-saw was the bit where the chief hijacker obligingly ushers me towards my car, saying 'sure, whatever you like, you just sit there and we'll hijack you', and then pulls his gun out of his ankle holster and starts loading it. *Loading* it, not unloading, and I'm pretty sure he doesn't keep a supply of blanks in his pocket for demonstration purposes. I say: hang on now are we not perhaps taking the spirit of verisimilitude a little far, or words to that effect. He says no, he wouldn't feel right hijacking me without bullets. The better part of valour overtakes me and I cede my seat to one of the other hijackers, one of a pair of twins, which is a relief because even though no bullets fly he acquires a batch of bruises in the course of the assault.

This episode brings up questions, the most common of which is: 'Were they real hijackers?'

Well, after the demo I said, 'You've done all this right on camera, don't you feel a touch shy?'

To which one guy laughed very loud and said, 'No, why should we worry? We're just showing you what we *think* the hijackers might do if there were any hijackers around.'

I said: 'And if they didn't find the driver sitting conveniently in the car, what might they do then?'

He said, promptly whipping a home-made tool from his pocket: 'Ah, we *think* they might have a thing like this and they would use it to do like this,' imitating the motion of breaking the doorlock.

Yes, they are real hijackers. What is more they are highly identifiable hijackers, operating under the aegis of a godfather who is a household name around Soweto. To thousands of Sowetans our whereabouts were as unhidden as the godfather's name, which I refrain from mentioning solely because Messrs Penguin Books will have penguinlets about the theoretical possibility of a libel suit. The godfather, a fellow of uncommon charm and personality, has been in the public eye since he was a young sports hero, and if you ask almost any Soweto citizen who is the Mr Big of the hijacking trade they'll name him without a pause.

Why then is he still at large? Dunno. After our programme I asked the police. They said (a) they can't bring charges against people for saying they're hijackers; they have to have a specific offence with a specific place, date, and victim, and (b) nothing anyone said to me counts legally as the speakers had not had their legal rights explained to them.

What, then, of the moralities? We go and hobnob with the perpetrators of particularly odious villainy. We even laugh with them, and part from them on apparently good terms. Is this right?

It gave me trouble. At that time and that place, one behaves civilly. Indeed, sometimes nervously, particularly at the end when tensions arose. I was aware that behind the amiable chat in the sun lay corpses and widows and orphans, and I said so, with vague responses from the hijackers. I know they ought to be in jail and I said that too. Some people felt I had glamorised them. I don't feel that, but I won't say that misgiving was absent.

There was an exchange on that day which I regretted was not on camera. A resident of nearby Dobsonville said she had been at a local meeting to discuss the crime problem. Everybody was anxious that the godfather should pitch up. He did. Speaker after speaker bemoaned the crime wave.

The meeting waited for the godfather to take a turn. Finally he stood up and strongly supported the thrust. All this crime was truly terrible, he said, and he would join the people and do his bit for law and order, 'just as long as nobody wants to interfere with my right to rob the whites'.

As she put it: 'We gave him a big cheer and said: 'Fine'.'

★ ★ ★

The programme where we met Deon and the taxi war was focused on the Flying Squad. The day we got there was the day the police demilitarised. As of midnight the old army-style ranks had been replaced by Inspectors and Superintendents. I arrived mid afternoon along with the night shift, guys whose total prior exposure to the new ranks had been in the small hours, hours during which their attention was susceptible to distraction. Everybody was calling everybody else by the new ranks.

They hardly missed a beat. The CO, Colonel Van Vuuren, was sommer straightaway Superintendent Van Vuuren. 'Superintendent' is not a word created by, for, or from Afrikaners. It's spelt the same which actually makes things worse; at least 'Inspekteur' and 'Direkteur', two other tortured imports, look different, so you're in no doubt when you meet them. Superintendent looks the same but sounds otherwise. The inflections are all wrong. The emphasis comes on the middle 'IN' and the final 'DENT' and the word is as jarring as a jackhammer. But these ouens were going at it like old pros. Not for the first time I thought that all that worn stuff about 'ingrained attitudes' is bull.

Then, somehow, up came the subject of the wapen.

'Wapen' can mean weapon but it can also mean badge, and in this case it meant badge. Technically it's called a 'mustering', I think, but everyone just uses 'wapen', an unsatisfactorily ambiguous term in more ways than one. A police full-dress tunic is full of wapens, of diverse brands.

The cops were talking about a particular wapen, though: the one that showed they belonged to the flying squad; a badge not yet 18 hours deceased.

Everybody had needle-holes in their shirts, where the badge had been. Everybody was livid. They had parted from their ranks without a cheep, but not their wapen, oh no. They were saying that without their wapen, for all anybody knew they could just be any old cop, dog squad or aliens unit or desk drivers or anything. They weren't special any more.

Over at the dog squad, to say nothing of Internal Stability or CID and wheresoever two or three policemen were gathered together, I have no doubt the same discussion was going on in the same tones but with different specifics.

Was this funny, or what? You take away the time-honoured, life-long vocabulary of their aspirations, and they say Yes, Sir. Or, any rate, Ja SuperINtenDENT. You take away an all but nameless piece of cloth, which the overwhelming majority of the citizenry never notices anyway, and they're ready to revolt. It wasn't only funny, though. It was sad too. They wanted that wapen, and they couldn't see why they couldn't have it. Me neither. For my money there's an alarm bell here, ringing loud.

The Boere rose to the big change, and rose extraordinarily. What happened to the mighty right-wing revolt that — it's hard to recall now — we were expecting even on the morning of April 27 1994? It evaporated before lunch, is what, and what was left went at high noon on May 10 when a black choir took the screen to sing Die Stem in Afrikaans from the Union Building steps.

As a nation we glid with amazing ease away from that moment of awe. Pity. It *was* a miracle. For 342 years the Boere had been growling 'It's *our* country.' Now all of a sudden they said to the rest of us, souties and darkies en almal: 'Oh, y'mean you *want* some? Ag, why didn't you *say* so?' This was a moment the like of which the world has seldom seen. Maybe it's natural that the beneficiaries of the Boere's turnabout respond by kicking them in the teeth all the time, over their language and their wapens and their modest requests for a bit of social space to call their own. But it's still a pity, in more ways than one, because these ouens are going to long remain the backbone of the nation, as I was re-reminded the night with the flying squad.

It started with a parade of sorts, police-style as opposed to military, with the incoming shift propping up the walls of a large bare classroom to be given a small hullo and a very low-key pep talk by a woman captain. Also a couple of minutes' equally low-key commiseration for Van der Merwe and Van Schalkwyk, both doing okay in hospital after yesterday's mishaps.

After the parade I asked some officers howcome (i) proceedings were 100% Afrikaans, and (ii) attendance was 96% white. The first answer was sweet, a nonplussed blinking assurance that er, well, that's what everybody speaks. The second was an answer I've heard many times in similar situations, viz: 'Oh, there are very few applications from Them for this high-risk stuff, and even when they do apply they don't usually make it.'

I have no doubt there is something in this answer. I have equally no doubt it is not a whole answer. If I'd been a township boy at that parade, English my second or third language and Afrikaans about my sixth or seventh, I'd have felt as alienated as a labrador in a pit-bull ring. It wasn't only the language either (and when it came to one-to-one conversations with the few blacks around, the Boere always switched to English). It was the whole vibe, which said to outsiders: 'You're outsiders.'

I as a guest was a very well-welcomed guest, and indeed as a guest I was again awed by that same miracle, by which I whom they once would have glowered at as a busybody and a kommunis, and who would have felt edgy and eerie in the lair of the fascists, was now appreciated and appreciative and at one with my hosts. But it's not the same for the guys who are in the team. If they're outsiders their outsideness is a feature, and much as the officers will be outraged by this observation, I am confident that it is real. Perhaps it is easier for a fresh pair of eyes to notice the different dynamics − the 'one of the boys' interaction versus the 'oh, passengers' interaction.

When I next hear a roomful of white policepersons tell me that they can't get black applications for the tough stuff, I'll listen, all right, and I'll accept most of the implication that the Boeresersante have a monopoly on insane bravery. But I'll also say: 'Well, until those other guys have a real slice of ownership of the process, you'll never get the applications.'

Along around dusk things were quietish and when two cops — a sergeant and a lady WO — went off to check out a death I thought I'd better go with them. Maybe nothing else was going to happen. The death was of an aged tramp, in the burgeoning new squatter camp where the old Johannesburg abattoir used to be.

This was a sad death, which I wish to say is not such a platitude as you might think. Some deaths are good deaths — right time, right circs, at the right end of a right life. I learned this lesson recently. It was the last lesson I learned from my father. But the death of a guy whose privates are hanging out of his rags, lying on a pile of garbage he'd been scrabbling through, his expiry so uncertainly different from his life that the neighbours spent a day thinking he was just drunk... nah, that's a sad death.

Then again, what the heck did it have to do with the flying squad? Here is meant to be the arm of the law at its terrifying quickest; ready to descend at a moment's notice on malfeasants in every unexpected part of this far-flung country. The flying squad was presumably no less understaffed than any other segment of our embattled police service, and here we were ambling around a harmless little squatter camplet, the police with their rifles casually crooked over their arms like English county squires at tea after a pheasant shoot, being saddened by a death?

I put this query to my two cops, and then to the ever-increasing number of plainclothes police (all, incidentally, black) who kept on arriving to fill in forms and scrutinise the corpse from varied angles. I wasn't getting much answer.

Suddenly there was a popping sound in the middle distance, and by the time I figured out it wasn't a mistimed Guy Fawkes party there was ol' Deon in full sprint to the action.

I got to the rank after Deon had done his single-handed occupation of it. It looked like a battlefield, figures lying around in various degrees of proximity to death's door, both sides of the door. Within ten, fifteen minutes the place was sewn up. Barriers all over, detectives detecting, informers informing, first aiders first aiding. The entire operation – it's perhaps odious to say but I say it because it was awfully evident – was run by Boere. I asked one guy with lots of pips where was the New SA presence in this. He jerked his head at a car, and said: 'There', and indeed in the car were two officers doing not much that was obvious. He was implying that they were staying in safety; I wondered as before whether this was a whole answer or whether there was an ownership-and-belonging factor here too. I don't know what the answer was. I do know that the visible evidence was a solid phalanx of white Afrikaners cleaning up a mess created by non-white non-Afrikaners, and I couldn't ignore that. One scene in particular showed a group of police paramedics frantically trying to save the life of an armed taximan who I had to assume might equally well have been among the shooters and not the shot, and this scene concentrated the mind fairly powerfully in a direction that had little to do with the old standard idea of a callous oppressive force ignoring black interests.

We did more that night with our policemen, including more of the stuff that raised questions about the usage and deployment of the flying squad, such as a lengthy completion of formalities in respect of a day-old suicide.

Around midnight we got back to headquarters, and I spent a long while wandering around the room. The range of actions and attitudes and types of incoming call was vast. There were people phoning to complain about noisy parties in the street. Then there was a woman saying: 'They're breaking the door now. They're smashing it with an axe. The door is splintering.'

Although there were various high-ranking characters around, the room was run by a young sergeant – Bester, I think – who was working up a heart attack trying to be in nine places at once. During a lull I asked him why he was running from point to point like an athlete, barking orders from one desk to one patrol car and then hurtling across the room to bark other orders at another car from another desk, rather than using the super-sophisticated electronic comms that were supposed to do all this at the touch of a button. 'Gee, man,' he said, 'some of this stuff is urgent, I haven't got time to wait for the systems.'

Somewhere along the way somebody blew his nut in Westbury and laid waste to a whole clutch of people. It was big news over the next few days. That massacre went on for quite a while, with call after anxious call coming through and Bester very nearly blowing his own nut in his fury to get reinforcements there instantly. If I'd been one of the callers I would have been furious too. I would have wanted to get hold of George Fivaz right then and there to complain angrily about this off-hand police treatment from guys who wouldn't even hear me out. I would have had no idea of Bester going crazy out of earshot, juggling demands and resources and priorities and screaming at this car and that one to get there *now*.

Among the constables at the phones there was every attitude imaginable. Some were happily assuring callers with tuppenny problems that 'yes, the police are on their way' despite knowing perfectly well there was nil chance. Others were painstakingly putting callers off, warning that it would take hours at minimum for their case to be attended to, and grimly tolerating the floods of invective and abuse that this truthful information elicited. One guy was laid back to the point of catatonia, driving Bester close to perpetrating his own crime of violence. Another was treating every call as if it came from his mother, and every delay as a personal affront.

I quit, eventually. I could do that thing. Say 'thanks guys, been an interesting evening', and take off to an inviting bed. The people I left there couldn't. Neither them nor their colleagues burning up the fisc's tyres and brakepads and their own personal private red corpuscles. I drove home in silence, eschewing even the company of the tape player. This was not the first time I had been disturbed by the contrast between the relative comforts and the relative worth to mankind of, on the one hand, the cosy dilettantes who footle about in media and similarly frivolous occupations, and on the other the sustainers of the thin blue line. Shouldn't think it's the last time either. And while I'm certainly not offering to swop I'll say this for free: If somebody rigs up a system whereby citizens could voluntarily increase their taxes to supplement a policeman's minuscule salary, count me in.

In terms of public response, the Deon scene and the hijack scene were the hits. Fine, you can't dictate taste to the public. I listen. I notice. I accept. I recognise that the next series and its (I hope) successors will have to also offer some of the cowboys-n-crooks stuff. But I hope not too much. Skop skiet en donder is a part of South African reality, but not the whole reality. Our business is to seek a whole. Back at the beginning Patrick Lee said something memorable. I paraphrase it as: 'When you get a series like this, it is because someone has bought a core idea. From then on everybody involved — marketers, advertisers, bureaucrats, and production people — will try to beat that core idea back. In your case the core idea is a skew view — an independent and unfettered perspective on what the nation is about. Never let it go.'

Right, Patrick.

10

Truth and its Enemies

Of the 46 Treks to date, I'd guess that some 30 have had the effect of leaving viewers feeling more cheerful about their country and its people. Another ten or so, neutral. The remaining six might just have added to the traffic at the immigration counters of the Western consulates.

Ratios like those, and the approach behind them, attract diverse criticisms. I get variously accused of being a closet Pollyanna given to pulling rose-tinted wool over public eyes, or of sabotaging the national quest to cultivate confidence.

Either version is fine by me. On this score there are no apologies in my conscience. The principle is untroubled: where there is good news I like to find it. Where there is the other thing, I hope I do not run away from it. That's not logically symmetrical, but it works in my head. It's a brand of balance, casuist as may be, and for my money this

interpretation of balance gives the Trek a certain value.

This is a time and place where balance gets pushed to the rear. There is on the one hand a New SA chest-beating cum cliché-mouthing — frenetic hurrahs for the new state and all its works. The hurrahs are accompanied by denunciation of criticism, by an inability to distinguish debate from treason or scrutiny from racism, and by an alacritous ascription of every fault and flaw to the hangovers of the old ways. There is a lemming element in this outlook, and I think it is an outlook in need of having its cage rattled.

Then again, it doesn't get under my skin in the same way as the opposite outlook, the one espoused by the Apostles of Misery, in comparison with which the politico-racial naivety of the NewSA mob is a downright attraction.

The Apostles are depressingly over-populous in the Engelse professiono-exec world that I live in, and are at their happiest when they're capping their neighbours' gloom stories. Nothing like gloom to give them a kick. A good gloom-chat is a thing anybody can climb into. It does not inconveniently require you to actually *know* anything, as if you were talking about software or aluminium or Bosnia or something. You just need to have confidentially heard some rumour of this or that cabinet minister being a hopeless corrupt drunk, or of the Reserve Bank being within one year or two months or three days or four hours or five minutes of irrevocable collapse, or of final proof that the nation's water supply is about to run out, and you can join right in and confidentially spread the same authoritative information to every passing ear that cares to hear.

The Apostles spend their days accumulating the evidence of decline, so that when they are gathered together they can be sure to have something to contribute to the litany of despair that, they can be equally sure, will be the basic fare of the social intercourse. They drive from the powergates of home to the sentry-check at the office with their heads down and their

137

windows up. They seethe and growl at the No-Job-No-Food mob cluttering up the stop-streets with pathetic placards. Watch through your rearview and you can see their blood-pressure rising as they angrily avoid noticing the gnarled destitute hand pleading for alms. You can see them mentally composing the next episode in their eternal wail about how the nation is sliding without trace into mid Atlantic.

A plague on both houses. If the roses-all-the-way fraternity are in dire need of a return to earth, the gloom brigade are in direr need of a boot to the bracket. The trick is to apply the boot in a way that gives heft to the skop, which disqualifies the traditional 'optimist' formula of 'look at our lovely beaches, look at our lovely weather, look at our lovely lions snoozing there under the tree, there, man, see, there's a tail flicking I think'. That stuff doesn't wash in a sub-culture dedicated to the proposition that next year the electricity will fail and the following year the black hordes will annex the garden gazebo.

It's a schizophrenic nation and it has a schizophrenic media. Look at what you might in shorthand call the newspaper formula by which the news media on the whole scurry unnoticing past any quantity of reasonable, normal, working activities for the sake of finding a pulse-quickening Blunder or Scandal headline. Look then at the magazine formula, where every biography is of a saint and every travel feature is of a paradise. Travel in particular is journalism's nemesis. Not so much that it is a trade built upon cliché ('Land of Contrasts' — aargh) but that the open sewer outside the hotel window, with which the writer regales every Sunday lunch for two years after, never gets mentioned in the copy. What does get mentioned, with all the subtlety of an axe, is the comfort of the sponsored airline seats, the road-eating prowess of the sponsored 4x4, and the flawlessness of the hotel chain whose fat ad just happens to be placed overleaf.

As I see the Trek it must speak to an audience partly Pollyanna, demanding relentless sunshine, and partly Cassandra, seeing a new catastrophe at every blink, and it must speak as an island within a media firmament substantially split into misanthrope and prostitute. I set out to speak to both gangs in the same breath, which puts credibility at quite some premium. I pursue credibility by the ultimately uncomplicated method of saying it like I see it, and most times what I see at first hand is less upsetting and/or more heartening than what one is told at second hand to expect to see.

A prime example was the race war at the Vaal Technikon. In autumn '95 this was heavy headlines, massively fortified by a much-replayed TV scene of an actual head-cracking bone-breaking glass-shattering racial battle in the campus quadrangle.

We got there as usual a day or two after the headlines began to shrink, meaning that the news teams had drifted off to some other place where the prospect of more and fresh broken heads was higher. Funnily enough, though, an unscheduled extra Vaal bout had come to the boil in the meantime and we, the only media mense in sight, walked right in to the opening skirmishes.

The campus is surprisingly large and grassy and in the middle of a wholesale upgrading. Its original buildings, cast in the jail-like mould of educational institutions, were and still are being overtaken by the ambitious development of a new-and-improved 90s-style neo-classical edifice. Thank heaven for the recovery of architecture.

The issue revolved around the person of the rector. Black students were saying that the rector was biased and crooked and they couldn't be expected to study properly until he was removed and democratic structures installed. White students suspected that the anti-rector line was a red herring by which the blacks sought to deflect attention from their classroom shortcomings. Moreover, they said, if there was a problem let it be sorted out by discussion etc instead of having boycotts obstruct their routes to careers.

In the middle of the campus there was a broad ditch which became the Rubicon. On the one side, furious Boerseuns armed with clubs and sjamboks declaring that if the blacks crossed there would be some very big bumps in heads. On the other side were angry blacks armed with uprooted fenceposts and projectiles picked from the hills of building rubble, saying ready or not we're coming. In the manner of dogs growling through a fence the bluster and taunting proceeded for quite a while, during which assorted leadership figures were doing the things that leaders do, threatening, cajoling, whipping up, calming down, and all of these in varying degrees.

It became evident that there was a main man on each side, these main men bearing the names Kingsley Boloang and Vleis van Tonder respectively. With Kingsley I spoke at length. Vleis ducked me assiduously, for the usual reason that leadership-type Righties believe that the media's mission in life is to shaft them. I spoke to plenty of other Boerseuns, though, and I was astounded by how inwardly unfierce they were behind the facade of truncheons, whips and shouted threats. In the circumstances I expected to hear the 'kaffirs off our campus' line. What I actually heard was a highly unexpected redolence of acceptance and even welcome: 'We have no problem with the black students being here, just that they put us through all this trouble because they want to invent imaginary complaints about our rector.' On the other side, the sounds were similar. Strange war when the combatants are outdoing themselves to be nice about the enemy.

The upshot was that after much orderly intervention by the police, a little added interference from some annoying TV busybody, and a summit conference at the ditch where Vleis, Kingsley and others initiated a drop-your-weapons move — *zoop*, in a surreal moment the aggro was all over and everyone sloped off to the canteen. It was almost as if tea-break had been called in a movie battle scene.

140

I was not at this time Mr Popularity among the SAP, and especially in the eyes of a colonel at whose peace-making strategies I had cavilled, but as the general tension simmered down so did the lowered eyelids of the lawmen de-lower and in a while the officers and I, left taking spacious sun on the ex-almost-battlefield, were chewing the fat like old chommies. Out of nowhere and to my great surprise the same colonel (whose manner of speaking to the blacks I had thought unduly curt) said: 'The blacks' complaints are quite right, you know. Just a pity that these white kids don't pay attention to those issues.'

Indeed if you found a category of youngsters who combined the socio-pol acumen of black SA youth and the textbook-and-technological vernuf of the whiteys, you'd conquer the world. With the officer's comment I at least felt we were conquering the race war. The last thing I'd expected was a provincial Afrikaner police chief taking the bolshie side of the row. Later several of the white technikon staff made much the same points (eventually borne out by the commission of inquiry).

When I returned to the wider world, where the Vaal Technikon was still in its five minutes of fame as a symbol of another step down the slippery slope, I was partly angry at the inadequacies of public information and partly uplifted by the reality I had found and the solubility it pointed to.

Here was a classic case of a common phenomenon. The world is told: eek, disaster. On the ground level, it's more a matter of finger trouble. The world is told: racial strife. On the ground level . . . well, yes, it is racial strife but it is also wildly more subtle than those two words convey.

Nearly a year later the Trek's 1996 run was beginning, and by way of a foreword to the broader audience of the new SABC3 we recapped some of the previous year's material, including the technikon.

As we re-cut the footage it occurred to me that it was an amazingly long time since the public prints had heard from that quarter. Obviously, that meant things were all right. When something is going horribly wrong you can be sure there's a camera pointing up every orifice. When all is calm and you wish to announce unto the nation: 'See, you got a wrong idea, *this* is what things are normally like', you can shriek your vocal organs into shredded carrot and nobody will hear you bar the next door neighbour, who calls the cops. If it ain't wrong, it ain't news.

So we pointed south, and we hit the campus, and we were met by a welcoming committee of vice-rector Prof Kotie Grove and two newly installed members of Council, Messrs Vleis van Tonder and Kingsley Boloang.

Serendipity is hardly the word. If we'd scripted it somebody would have had to edit it out as too romantic. Walt Disney would barely have the chutzpah to abruptly convert the two chief adversaries to lovebirds, yet there they were, colleagues and friends, and here was the apotheosis of the good-news story. On a balcony overlooking the scene of the erstwhile head-cracking, Kotie and Kingsley and Vleis tell me earnestly how well everybody is now getting on. That is what viewers see, and in light of my suspicion that viewers will be sceptical, I go into a song-and-dance about it being a genuine case of the truth that is stranger than fiction.

Fine, lekker, big step forward. What the viewers did not see were the subsequent subtleties. I wandered round the campus and heard a lot of worries: foreign students, mainly Zairean and Congolese, on their shabby treatment at the hands of the locals and the non-recognition of French; local black students on being held back by Zaireans who couldn't speak English, on the alleged re-capture of student affairs by whites, and on the effort by some teachers and some classes to still use 50% Afrikaans. From the white students, worries about having to have 50% of their tuition in English, on feeling like strangers at student meetings, and, most of all, on not learning enough.

Are they learning enough or are they not? How true or untrue the belief is, how much it varies from course to course and place to place, must be a contender for Crucial Question Number One, even in a time not short of crucial questions. That there is such a dearth of public discussion on such a giant source of private concern is hard to believe. Is this what political correctness means – 'duck the hard issues'?

White students commonly believe that they're learning less than their elder brothers learned, because today's teachers are teaching at slower pace and lower level to accommodate the blacks. The great majority of 'historically white' places of learning being now largely black, one result is the emergence of a new breed of historically non-existent private campus whose unstated sales case is: 'The way for fee-paying properly-prepared students to acquire top-level expertise unhampered by floundering classmates or trashed campuses'.

You can understand the incentive. The campus-trashing thing is so primitive that when you see it in lewende lywe you genuinely wonder for a bewildered moment whether you've slipped your drivebelt. People who you might have known as reasonable individuals are suddenly a jeering gloating mob taking bizarre delight in strewing vrot fruit and splats of old yoghurt through corridors. Watch that for a while and after getting over the initial sensation of disbelief you progress to the next sensation, which is startlingly clear and is also universal. What you think as you watch is: 'For my children's tertiary education I must find somewhere where there are no blacks'.

If you think that's harsh, you've never been at a trashing. I'd love to hear of any single parent, of any colour, who has watched a campus-trashing under way and has not thought exactly that. My first trashing experience was in fact in the company of a very black parent, Nomavenda Mathiane, who is full of sympathy for Azapo's dedicated blackness and the PAC's Africa-for-the-Africans, and she said exactly that (although she did add the thoughtful rider 'until the blacks stop having to prove themselves'). Being an honest person even before she is a political animal, she's one of the few who'd say it in public as well as in private. Most people say it in very extreme terms in the one context and get bashful in the other.

However you express it, the fact is that while you watch a trashing you are seeing the trashers as sub-human. You might restore them to humanity five minutes later, when they're behaving like humans again and maybe some of them are having a real impact upon you, talking about their pressures and worries and desperation, but at the time you can't believe that actual two-legged members of the species homo sapiens are purposefully making filth. What you can believe is that they're doing wonders for the shares of the private campuses.

Add to the trashing the factor of floundering classmates, and you see that private education is the growth industry of the next decade. In the old, white, days you might have had one student in twenty so far out of it that it was unfair to have admitted him, and the poor ou would be left to sink on his own. Now one in maybe five or seven black students is in that position, and that becomes a brake. On Trip Two to the Vaal Technikon some very gripping stuff along these lines came up as I talked to students.

Did it come up on the public screen? No, it did not.

Why not? The aforementioned combination of reasons — sight vs sound vs content; spontaneity vs camera; editors vs exhaustion & wives & girlfriends & uneaten dinners & unused movie tickets. So having discovered a real good-news story with a large number of qualifiers, riders, and catch-clauses, all that we gave the public was the good-news bit and I was left to come away with a lonely set of doubts and cautions.

Such things happened. They still happen. Am I apologising? No, I'm asserting that the good/bad up/down thing is too confused to get it close to straight through that unsubtle medium the video camera. Sometimes the up side is the up of a glimpse, a laugh, a smile, sometimes the up of energy and effort and honesty and decency. It is rarely the up of graphs and statistics.

Statistics or no statistics, for my money the soft ups can take you a long way up and I am happy to project them even when the projection is an incomplete projection. Ideally you want to project the snares and traps as well, but when you can't get them across you can't get them across. Incomplete projection is not the object but it's not illegitimate either. What is illegitimate is false projection, which is a different thing. If I'm seeing a truth before my eyes I'll say I'm seeing it. Without exception, it is less than a whole truth. If it's a long way less than a whole truth that's a pity, but as long as it's nothing but the truth it's passable.

You think this is self-evident? Obvious? I gently demur. I am making a point that has hit me only through the doing of the Trek, a point which passed me by through half a life as a consumer and practitioner of public information. It is that the big gap is not between truth and half-truth, but between the quest for truth and the quest for something else, such as the quest to make people feel good (à la the NewSA propagandists) or the quest to make people feel bad (à la the Apostles, who seek company in their own worries and reassurances for their own misgivings).

Lately I have been exposed to numerous scripts for advertisements and for that tortured neologism 'infomercials', which bring the difference home. These things are not looking for a truth. They are designed to promote a message. The truth is relevant only as far as you must retain a connection with it to make the message believable. You can't say 'our new smoke-stack filters are 100% effective', because you will be widely disbelieved and risk being easily disproved. So you say what you believe the market will bear, treating truth as an opinion survey. I was at one point invited to put my voice and my face on a screen to announce precisely that a certain new filtering device was 95% effective. Privately, the promoters didn't even blink about telling me they were battling to crack the 50% rate.

Before the Trek I had, as a reader and viewer and listener of the media, taken a bit of advertising hyperbole in my stride. On 702 I had also, although sometimes with a raised eyebrow, read out advertisements which would be widely taken as unexceptionable: 'If you register at X College you'll get a good job', 'If you take Y pills you'll feel strong and young' etc.

But the Trek experience and its constant wrestle with the notions of truth, non-truth, half-truth and incomplete truth, has turned me into an unapologetic bundle of neuroses on this subject, and something of a missionary freak. You may say if you wish that I take myself over-seriously here, but I've learned that there are people, not necessarily many people, often very unsophisticated people, to whom I, by virtue of the nature of the Trek, fill a role as tourguide of thought and busdriver of opinion. They believe that if I say a thing that means I mean that thing, and I'm not going to let those people down even in the little ways that I might have done before the Trek made me hyperconscious of the issue. Never not no more am I ever saying anything I don't mean. Nooit. I take it to extremes. I don't even say 'nice dress' or 'you're looking lovely' if I don't mean nice dress or you're looking lovely. (Fortunately my family womenfolk look lovely to me pretty much all the time.) And on air, extremer extremes. I compensate for the frustrating inaccessibility of the whole truth by placing an acute premium on nothing but the truth.

And by truth I do not claim an objective truth. It's about subjective honesty. If I utter a word or sentence that inwardly I do not mean, that's wrong. But as long as what I am saying is true to what I do mean, I exonerate myself for the depths that I leave out. You can and must aim to cover the issue from A – Z. You know that the best you can possibly achieve is actually about F or H, and in practice you are very seldom going to get beyond C or D. You can't weep about the Ks and Ts and Vs and Ys that you don't get to. You can't even kick yourself; not with good effect at any rate. All you can usefully do is make sure that right as far as you go, the B, the C, the E with luck, you offer as honest a perception as your limited lights permit.

In this spirit, would somebody kindly explain to me how to deal with the SA ethnic concatenation?

As a rule, where the Africans screw up they screw up in clear and visible and conspicuous ways such as their inability to keep public places clean. Where the whites screw up, it's subtle and insidious and hard to define.

Thus for instance: I'm wandering around Soweto, looking for landmarks. The programme is on landmarks or, more broadly, on the goods and the bads of Johannesburg's urban architecture. We've 'done' Joburg proper, and now want to incorporate the broader city. Some deep-died Sowetans are composing the route. They're having a bit of difficulty finding landmarks. With few exceptions the places they take us to are mainly distinguished by having been burnt down in or after 1976.

We get to Pace College, the so-called Soweto Michaelhouse, which is encouraging enough in human terms — we speak to a terrific class of sharp, on-the-ball senior students — but landmark-wise is no great shakes. The grounds are shrunk to a fraction of their original size, as people keep stealing the fences and encroaching on the fields. The sports facilities are derelict. The lawnmower has evidently been lost since 1906.

We get to the Oppenheimer tower, in the middle of a park in the middle of Soweto, which only one of our escorting party has ever been to. Most of the others have never noticed it. One, who has lived a kilometre away since birth, says he always thought it was 'something for whites', and indeed the park's main function has been as a teatime stop for visiting foreign dignitaries. While we're there a heavy police escort brings in a group of uniformed Commonwealth army officers.

We get to Regina Mundi, the 'political cathedral', which is a landmark all right, and large, and marked by nicks in the walls caused mainly by police bullets and holes in the roof caused mainly by wear, but is also so conspicuously unambitious in comparison with the great spired 13th century classic cathedrals that one is deterred from making too much of it.

Then we get to Phefeni station, which, we are assured, is a real new landmark, wholly unique. The uniqueness turns out to be that the station is specially designed to make gang wars difficult and police encirclement easy. In this purpose it appears to have worked, but this is not your ideal, emotion-tugging brand of landmarkery. Most of the place, other than under the sides of the bridge, is ankle deep in litter. Under the sides of the bridge is neck deep in litter.

I buy the congregation Cokes and hot dogs, with difficulty as the hot dog shop is trying hard to set a Soweto record for incompetence, and we retire to a balcony at the station where an excellent argument ensues about the humane inefficiency I find at the hot dog shop compared to the inhumane efficiency the others encounter looking for the same purchase on the white side of town at what they still call the Greekshops (the term everybody used when I was a kid but which has since been sensitised into disfavour in white society).

This debate goes somewhere. It's a fine debate and in its way pathbreaking. Unfortunately it is also all over the place, with numerous freelance participants joining in, and Louis is doing calisthenics trying to get his boom from side to side to catch each new spontaneous remark without catching Richard's standard muttered 'boom's in shot'. The inevitable result is that the tape picks up only the second half of each sentence. At the edit-suite later hours of painstaking cutting distil only a shadow of the real discussion.

Somewhere along the way one of the main guides casually tosses his cooldrink can onto the station concourse. I blow up, and yell at him about civic responsibility. A new and hotter debate springs forth. Somebody says what business is it of mine, this is their place. I say it's part of my country. Somebody else says there is already so much mess on the ground that one more can makes no difference. I say the mess is because leadership figures like him legitimise mess. Somebody else says the authorities don't provide bins. I walk, while the camera follows, from bin to bin to bin, half of them emptier than the ground around them. My guides drop their argument in a mass of good-humoured if slightly hysterical giggles.

Well, this is TV. It's active, it's visual, it's short sharp sentences, it's 1 000% unscripted, it's real. It even has that rare bonus, unrehearsed fun and laughter. What is more the great bulk of it happens to be audible, for no profounder reason than the accident that numerous successive comments are made by people standing near one another rather than people standing on the other side of the group.

So it features on the screen, and for months to come I have Soweto people referring to it; some on my side, some on the others' side, some saying they had a good laugh.

And also, not a few saying 'Why bash us, why not bash the whites?'

Aha, here's an interesting question, raising a salvo of its own interesting questions. Does an even-handed treatment of South Africa require that if a Khumalo comes in for criticism in one breath a Van der Merwe must get the same in the next? Would it be better to avoid criticism altogether, and go for the confidence-generating formula which may or may not have a beneficial impact upon dull minds at the expense of sacrificing credibility upon acute minds? Alternatively, does the health of the new nation demand adherence to the new nation's happy habit of ladling all criticism on the relics of the past? Or does one say: 'Sorry, but actually the whites are on the whole an organised bunch who provide the engine of South African progress, and now in the post-oppressive age there is not that much to criticise'?

Tricky. On the one hand there is an uncomfortable truth in the engine-of-progress attitude. It is not coincidence that the country with 60% of the continent's white people also delivers 60% of the continent's industry, electricity, communications etc.

Does this make the whites the angels of the equation? Not that I see. What I see is wholesale failure of the whites to respond adequately to Africa. That's bad enough. For me, what is worse is that it is a failure I can't reflect on the screen. It's subtle, soft, nuanced... television's nightmare.

Almost everywhere the Trek takes us, we come across the phenomenon of belittlement. Rarely is it a deliberate, purposeful belittlement. It is the belittlement of neglect or the belittlement of complacency. It expresses itself in scores of varied ways, but it always boils down to an assertion of white hegemony and black followership. For example:

● There is a manager going on and on about how holy and patriotic he and his company are. Two minutes later, camera off, we're walking through the factory. A black guy politely stands aside for us at a door. The manager doesn't notice him, doesn't acknowledge, nothing.

We come to a work-station. Mr Manager wishes to show a certain operation, so simply takes the controls from the hands of the man doing it, no please, no thankyou, no d'you mind, no nothing.

We come to another operation, where Mr Manager needs the participation of the operator. He barks an order. His voice changes as he barks it. It's not the way he's been talking to me. It's not the way he'd talk to the supervisor. It's the way he talks to the blacks. It's so natural he doesn't notice it.

If I say, as is difficult to say, 'Hey, that's not a nice form of address', he doesn't know what I'm talking about. He thinks I'm super-sensitive-bleeding-heart. He knows his people. He's not racist. He's stainless Model of Courtesy when the Provincial Minister of Trade comes for lunch. But when he's speaking to the machine-boy, which is the term he uses, the term that somewhere in the recesses of his cranium he knows is belittling, he speaks the way machine-boys get spoken to.

Not to me, certainly not to the camera, but to his peers and his family, he says things like 'Tsk, such a pity the blacks aren't up to it'. He's quietly certain that *he* is a contributor to the nation and *they* are essentially drains on the nation. For my money he is part of the problem.

• I'm at a prominent NGO. I'm interviewing two people: the chairman, being the black face which makes things seemly, and the chief executive, being the white face which makes things happen.

Ostensibly, the chief exec is deferentially standing back for his chairman to answer the questions. The chairman's English is hesitant. He is not a hands-on chairman, which is a weasel way of saying there are features of the organisation about which he knows radically less than a chairman should know. However, the word 'SINCERITY' is carved all over his face in pillars of granite, and the fullness of his good intentions is inspiring to behold.

At every turn — *every* turn — the CEO adds a rider to what the chairman says. He does not interrupt; does not contradict; does not gainsay; nothing so crass. He's a liberal, after all. At least, he would have called himself a liberal in the time when liberal was the benevolently respectable thing to be. Now that it has become contentious he would worry about the label, but he dines out on his services to the Cause. So he does not rebut his chairman. Oh no! What he does is, he *clarifies*.

That, anyhow, is how he would see it. How I see it is: he castrates.

That's an odd word to apply to one male's behaviour towards another male. It is a word more commonly associated with a hardline female feminist's behaviour towards a male (and it is not tautologous to specify *female* feminist. It is as possible for a male to be feminist as for a white to have been liberationist, and as sensible).

But castration is the word that impinges upon my mind as the CEO clarifies what the chairman says.

If it's a figure, and the chairman says the budget is a million rand, the CEO politely clears his throat and says: 'Ahem, one point one million.' If the chairman says the budget is one point one million rand, the CEO politely clears his throat and says: 'Ahem, one point one three million.' If it's geography, and the chairman says 'northern Mpumalanga', the CEO politely clears his throat and says: 'Ahem, northern and portions of eastern Mpumalanga.' If I had asked what the moon was made of and the chairman had said 'blue cheese', the CEO would have politely cleared his throat and said 'Ahem, with a tinge of Roquefort.'

What does one say to this guy? You can't tell him he's a depressing odious racist git. He would genuinely think you have a case of mistaken identity. Dammit, he's *committed*. He dedicates his life to the uplift of the disadvantaged. He earns half what he could earn in normal business. Without him, this NGO would be lame and useless.

True, too true. But without him the chairman might also grow balls.

- Etcetera.
- Etcetera.

Experiences like these come up all the time. Once in that blue moon the belittlement is manifest. Mostly it is disguised, even from the belittler's own conscious mind. In my belief this outlook bears as much responsibility for the morass of black ineffectiveness as does the flinging of junk onto station concourses by black leaders. Just one tiny problem: how, presenting the Trek, do I reflect this belief?

I don't, other than in piffling sidelong ways such as pulling up people who talk of adults as 'boys' or 'girls'. The crux is too intricate.

As I see it the most fundamental of all the fundamental needs in South Africa is the need for the people of South Africa to feel good about themselves. I don't mean 'good' as in 'hubris', the cocky sense that they are best and others are flawed. I mean 'good' as in the confidence that they have worth, they are needed, they have a role, they have a future.

In that sense, you want the feeling of feeling good to be very liberally spread around. Everybody ought to have it, and that is not just for altruistic reasons. It is also for reasons of hard selfish practicality. If you give whites the message: 'You guys are the salt of the earth and those other fellows are also-rans', you end up with a little island of embattled white prosperity amid a sea of black resentment. If you try the opposite trick — 'Shame, you poor blacks have been done down from beginning to end so be angry until 85% of neurosurgeons and actuaries and civil engineers are blacks and one in eight domestic gardeners is white, and by the way did you know that Pythagoras and Charlemagne and Marx were really black' — you end up with Zambia. In fifty years time your grandchildren will curse your memory and beg the Boere to come back from Argentina.

Plenty of the messages floating around today's South Africa are one-way messages, treating the nation as a racial contest. I want to get past that. I want us to get beyond it, but not at the cost of sham and falsity. In the end, the route beyond lies in the core of the doubly-derided liberal philosophy. It lies in treating people as individuals and not as representatives of race groups. You look at the person and not at the shade of the skin or the shape of the nose. You recognise honesty where you find it, sincerity where you find it, expertise where you find it, humaneness where you find it, surmounting the inducement to chain it to this or that presumed group characteristic.

Not in this generation's lifetime, though, and I wonder about the next, is this nation or this planet going to achieve the liberal apotheosis. There is no problem re the direction. The direction is fine. In the way that we have already gone nine tenths of the distance to eradicating the chains that once branded whites, in each others' eyes, as English or Afrikaans or Jewish, so are we proceeding in respect of the broader unchaining. In not long the confines of Colouredness or Indianness will have also evaporated. Person to person, in terms of one-to-one relationships, the same increasingly applies to Blacks. But all these are foothills. The mountain is the aggregated public relationship between Blacks and Others, and the nation is nowhere in sight of dusting its hands off after that particular climb.

To approach it, my method places a premium on straight talk and honest talk. Naturally that method invites the gauntlet of condemnation expressed by the parrot cry: Racist! Racist! Which is why it is the custom for straight talk to take place solely among consenting, and usually monochrome, groups in private (abundantly including black groups, where the flavour of private discussion is a world removed from the public rhetoric).

The gauntlet has long ago ceased to worry me. I get called racist about as often as I get called one of the various opposite epithets ('pro-black!' 'radical!') and the main effect is to liberate me from wasting effort on minds manacled by slogan. Race and race consciousness remains at the heart of the South African riddle, and patriotism as I understand it does not consist of trying to wish yourself into a purer world.

The Trek is an imperfect forum for refined social exploration, and the Big Questions do not often sneak their way in. Nonetheless there is an intellectual basis to what I think we ought to be doing there: aiming for a target and applying a method.

The target is a South Africa which works for its whole citizenry, and works for the soul as well as the stomach.

A chicken in every pot would be a tasteless chicken if the price was a sense of resentful inferiority. Conversely the satisfactions of liberatory chest-beating would be hollow if the price was the slippery slope to a second Zambia.

The method is straight talk. We've been through one big distortion, the one that said race was sacred at all costs. Now we're into another; the one which says change is sacred at all costs.

The Trek's business is to encourage change where change is progressive and question change where change means decline. We need the sense of representivity to be real, not bogus, and lasting, not fleeting. We need the sense of God in his heaven and all right with the world to apply to South Africans across the board, today, tomorrow, and thereafter. Perpetual query and perpetual needling is part of the route.

11
Ah! Afrika! Aargh!

From the start of the series there was a subtle bottom line, a core question: how fareth Africa? It was fine and well to look at the trappings inherited from the despised former state — the navy, disciplined and orderly if shrinking; the air force, effective if financially strapped; prisons, neat and clean if over-crowded. It was fine and well to divert into the peripheries of the social thoroughfare — art, vibrant and go-ahead even if the galleries echo to solitary footsteps; homes for the disabled, inspiring albeit imperfect and short-handed. But there is a single large dominant worry in the minds of South Africa's people. It is a worry way up forefront in the minds of the disaffected disporing to Perth and Toronto and Leicester and Pittsburgh. It is a worry gnawing insistently at the minds of their peers who grin inwardly when Canada freezes over or Britain has a car bomb spate. It is a worry that not a lot of black people are prepared to raise in public until after at least two beers. It is the worry that says: do we, too, wind up as a dreg in the cup of nations?

If you're sensitive on this account, skip this chapter. The surface-scratching into African Africa that we have done on the Trek has kicked me like a mule. From a Johannesburg armchair I had been happy to take the view: 'Hang loose, we'll muddle through.' Prior samplings from holidaying and journalising around the neighbour states hadn't overly dented that view either. The Trek knocked it into a cocked hat.

It's not, I protectively repeat, that the Trek has been a comprehensive explorer of the continent. It's that the fraction we have explored sounds alarm bells too loud to be ignored.

In three particular places the alarm bells clanged painfully.

From Zambia I came away with one overwhelming impression: these guys were hoaxed.

Thirty years ago they were told: 'Here, lucky people, freedom!' Thirty years later freedom is a charade. Hardly anything works and anything that does work works because it has been recolonised.

Lusaka's biggest landmarks are two gaunt half-buildings summarily left to decay when the Chinese pulled out five years ago. Pretty well everybody will tell you that the chief industry is dealing in cars stolen from South Africa. In so far as there are signs of movement, it is the re-colonisation movement. Ordinary Zambians point with happiness to the stirrings and say things like 'the Zambian supermarket went down but now there is a new one run by Lebanese', and 'the Zambian bus company went down but now there is a new one run by Greeks', not to mention that the Zambian brewery 'went down' but has now picked up majestically and is run by South Africans.

The beer is called Mosi wa Tunya, smoke that thunders, after the Chibemba for Victoria Falls. To everybody it is familiarly known by its first name, as any self-respecting three-word beer must expect to be. To the Zambians the Mosi has a short 'o', as in 'this Mosi is off'. To the expats it's pronounced with a long

Western 'o' like what a Jewish dentist is called by his friends. Until very recently what you would do when you drank a Mosi (which mainly meant you couldn't get a Castle) was pour it into a clear glass, hold the glass to the light and shake it, fish out foreign bodies and drink the rest. Lately Mosi has been recolonised by SA Breweries, the same instrument of oppression from whose grasp it was wrested thirty years ago, and if there is one single consistent message from the menfolk of Zambia it is the message: hooray hooray the beer's okay.

Practically nothing else is okay, other than that bulwark redeeming feature of Africa, the ubuntu of the people. Critical whites are used to scoffing at the notion of ubuntu, which they see as a flam attempt to invent something to stock the plus side of a scale overwhelmingly outweighed by balls-ups. Actually, ubuntu doesn't deny that Africans are as capable as anyone, if not more so, of murder, rape, pillage, arson, mayhem, manslaughter and tax evasion. It does say that in untroubled times everybody is everybody's friend. You meet people not by being ritually introduced through a mutual acquaintance as approved by Jane Austen and Wasp etiquette. You meet people then and there, by being there, and while you're there they're all your friends. That's ubuntu, and it is real, and if you open yourself to it it can give you extremely great rewards, which is handy because the practical side of life is apt to give you the opposite.

There are two economies in Zambia. There is what I term the Steakhouse Economy, which encompasses the 30 000-odd expats and maybe an equivalent number of Zambians, mainly civil servants. And there is the Stonecrusher Economy, which makes your stomach feel very strange indeed in a weird combination of despair and pride. You despair, or I do anyway, that so many people live so abjectly. You swell with pride that they retain the ubuntu despite their circumstances.

In the steakhouse economy there is one item of currency, the 500 kwacha note. This is the only item of currency. It is the highest note ever issued by the Zambian treasury, and it is the one and only sight of Zambian money that you ever see on the regular tourist circuit. It is worth R1,98, give or take. To host a steakhouse meal, take a sack. Be prepared, also, for a very long process settling the bill. Your steakhouse will have an automatic note-counter, which it will not use because the second chief industry is the inserting of brown paper inside piles of K500 notes. What is more you can't just give them the sack and say 'count it out', because (a) they haven't the management manpower and (b) they are used to this procedure leading to dispute ('Here's your sack back, sir.' 'What! There were at least a million kwachas in here and now it's almost empty!').

On the other side of town, in fact on every side of town, are the stonecrushers.

The first stonecrushers I met, I felt timewarp. But for the deceased automobile cabs, it could have been a scene from a prehistoric movie. It was a long straight road where you could see forever, and what you saw forever was two lines of the cabs of wrecked cars, one on each side of the road, with people sitting next to them breaking stone. The wrecked cabs are the stonecrushers' shops. That's what they call them, with not a hint of wryness. They're their shops, and they're proud of them. They've gone to a lot of trouble to break off the roofs of crashed vehicles and bring them here to be shops. From here they sell stone.

And to buy stone, you do not need to trade in K500 notes. The stonecrusher economy recognises not only K200 and K100 and K50 notes, but also coins, and once you get down to the one kwacha coin, value approx one third of an SA cent or one fifteenth of a US cent, you need not stop because you are still coming to ngwee, Zambian cents.

There are people who know Zambia well and who tell me, no, ngwee have long since ceased to exist. I don't know how to explain this. Maybe it's that they no longer exist in the eyes of the banks. What I do know is that in stonecrusher territory I found ngwee.

159

I purchase a sweet from a roaming vendor with a cardboard neck-tray. He wants 10 ngwee, a price which I inexpertly assess as equivalent to perhaps 2% of the smallest coin extant in the First World. The vendor is a very pleasant young man of about 25, with excellent English and first-class conversation. My supply of 10 ngwee coins being a touch low, I peel one of my steakhouse notes from the wad. When he starts scrabbling through his pockets trying to make up K499,90 change I feel sick. I tell him to keep the change and give him a few more notes to boot, thus for the first and I hope last time in my life administering to a service-provider a tip of 2,000,000% the cost of the service provided.

From a distance that might sound like fairy godmotherism. Close up, you feel nothing like noble or generous, you feel terrible. We know about wage-gaps, but this is cosmic gap. As timewarp, though, it was mild compared to the police station in the market.

We walked through one of the numerous Lusaka markets in the company of the highly encouraging and well-christened young editor of the Zambia News, Bright Mwape, whose name you have subsequently seen quite a lot, although it may not have registered. The SA press has taken an interest in Bright and his colleague Fred Mmbembe doing the revolving door at Lusaka Central for publishing wrong things in their News.

Bright was informative and thoughtful and amiable and very laid-back until I suggested that in the interests of doing as the Zambians do we might share a meal of the unnameable foodstuffs on offer at the eats section, at which he recoiled in shock and said if I really wanted to eat that stuff I should rather take it home and eat it within access to a South African hospital.

Bright had a fair-minded outlook on the life and times of his nation. While he weighed in the sacks on the government in respect of its effectiveness, he was strong on how the place was at least free these days. (After the dramatic changes of the last few months, I doubt he'd say the same now.)

When we came to the market police station, a largish shack with a tiny squeeze-in door, he said he had better call in and let the commander know that we were there. Surprised, I asked how the need to report our presence in a public place reconciled with all the freedom he'd been describing. He said no problem, just a courtesy call, as the commander would be wondering what was going on. Figuring that freedom can take very varied forms, I squeezed with him through the door.

The charge office was dank and dark, and it took me a while to adjust to a surreal sight. Behind it was a steel container, designed to transport goods, crammed to the gills with naked men.

These were prisoners, or detainees if you like. It was a hot summer day, and if the container was closed they fried. So the police had left the door open whilst prudently stripping the prisoners to quell the allure of the wide open spaces. We had a cheerful chat with the police captain, who drew the line at the camera seeing his prisoners but was unabashed by their treatment. It was simply humanitarian, he said. They were also people, after all. Fair enough, although the mind boggles at the thought of a Captain Van der Merwe trying to argue that case to the human rights watchdogs.

I came back from Zambia with a more stringent view of Africa than the one I'd gone with. I'd been uncritically contented with the muddle-through line: there'd be glitches and snafus and cock-ups, our own peculiar African glitches in addition to the standard human ones, but it would all come right in the end. After Zambia I felt No, this is cruel. They had thirty years of Zambianising and they went thirty years backward, everything stalling except the birth-rate. Now there is a new generation to whom it is axiomatic that if you want things to work you get the Lebanese or the Greeks or the South Africans in.

We, I suppose, are at about Year 4 of that cycle — the stage where Priority I is for the corridors of power to look representative. If you can find a black guy to become Chief

Exec, trumpet it from the rooftops. All concerned know that in nine cases out of ten the Chief Exec is not performing a chief executive job, but we're all so anxious to see the nation reflected in the decision-making arena that we put our finger on our lips. I don't think we can. I think we can and should adjust and adapt and compromise in a million ways, most of whose specifics are not yet fully or at all vouchsafed to us, but there is one vast no-go area. We can't monkey with the economy. We can't compromise the basic need to hone the cutting edge of wealth creation everywhere and in every way possible. Perversely, that is the thing with which we monkey the most. We play musical chairs in the small circles of privilege while our version of the stonecrusher world grows apace in the vast circles of indigence.

One of yesterday's papers as I write had a report headlined 'White Managers Remain in Charge'. It is a 12 paragraph story of which 11 paragraphs deal with the problems of affirmative action as reflected in the finding that the number of black senior managers has risen by only 0,4% over the last four years.

The 12th paragraph says: 'The number of white professionals has decreased by 15,3% since 1993 and a further decline of 32,4% is expected over the next three years.'

Today there is an anguished leader article agonising over the 0,4 figure and wholly ignoring the 15,3 and the 32,4.

Pass over the fact that all three of the figures involved are transparent rubbish, the first two being at complete variance with the evidence of the naked eye (below reality and above reality respectively) and the last a scare-mongering thumbsuck made ridiculous by the attempt to refine it to a decimal point. That is par for the course. Contemplate rather the proportions of concern. The unavoidable implication of an X% decrease in the nation's white professionals is an almost-X% decrease in the nation's product. Tsk, not worth mentioning. Rather worry about finding names that begin with M and end with vowels to legitimise the letterhead. If we want to get South Africa moving, creating, employing, send the executive classes, black and white, for a week in Zambia.

Zambia was upsetting in one way; Transkei in various others.

We were there with Jay Naidoo, shortly before the government splatted vanishing cream over its previously holy Reconstruction and Development Programme, of which Jay was Minister. We thought we were there to gauge the progress of RDP projects, and so did Jay. But this was in the run-up to the nation-wide local government elections (bad idea; staggered local elections would magnify parish pump issues and defuse national affiliations) so it wasn't really Jay's fault that he was press-ganged into service as ANC electioneer. Moreover, although he was the highest-ranking official around he was being hosted by various national and provincial departments other than his own, and I do not blame him for the low farce that ensued.

The trip was wrong in a thousand ways, starting with its conception. Maybe I'm an outdated Victorian at heart, but it does seem to me that when politicians are being politicians — that is, drumming up votes for their party — their party must pay for their time and their travel. If that politician is also a minister then when he is being a minister, ie working at least in theory for the greater good of the nation as a whole, fine, I the taxpayer am happy to provide his petrol.

Here we had pomp, glory, paraphernalia, and expense to excess. May I repeat that word with emphasis: *excess*. May I re-repeat it with bells, whistles, trumpets, and banners:

We start off with a military jet at Waterkloof. Waiting for Jay, and then waiting with Jay for part of his party, we take in the Highveld dawn, we take in a bracing walk across the runway, and we take in the VIP lounge. The visitors' book is a who's who, with names like Mandela, De Klerk, Mbeki, Gore, and some tannie called Elizabeth who couldn't remember her surname so she sommer put 'R'. We oblige with our own contributions: Ndlovu, Grealey, Dlamini, Beckett. (So isn't this meant to be a democracy, or what?) We fly in noisy leather opulence to Bisho airport. So far so good.

At Bisho we are met by an escort and a motorcade. Ja well okay, I don't expect Jay to stand at roadside raising finger for taxi. But then, nor do I expect the collected resources of the Eastern Cape provincial government to be marshalled around taking us to tea.

The Premier, Raymond Mhlaba, awaiteth. So we are told. The cups are laid out and the kettle is aboil. We hit the road, like the Wehrmacht invading Stalingrad. We bring all movement on our route to a standstill.

This is democracy? That The People overheat their radiators in furious hooting queues while The People's traffic department devotes itself to staving The People off lest the Hon Minister be delayed a valuable moment by their peasant presence?

In the earliest days of independent Zambia I stayed for a while on Independence Avenue, between State House and the Secretariat. Four times a day — Kaunda went home for lunch — the road was barred off. At first, impressionable dumb kid, I thought 'gee! power! important!' When I'd heard from the commuters and deliverymen and contractors who cooled their heels while the sirens squealed, the gee turned to ugh, the power to ash and the importance to vainglory.

Not long afterwards I was stuck in a traffic jam in London. Edward Heath, prime minister, was in the back of an elderly Humber next to me, fuming visibly. There was a profound revelation in this: that a society where the leaders get stuck in jams is a fundamentally better place than a society where they cause jams.

So what am I doing thirty years later jamming Kingwilliams-town in the name of none other than the ANC, The People's Movement and Restorer of Dignity? Dunno.

We are late, naturally, but if it matters it is not so you'd notice. Mhlaba greets his guests with hearty affability, coming across – it happens so often – as far more personable and pleasant in a handshake context than you expect from the TV image.

About 60 people – 12 or so from our flight and the rest locals, including journos, NGO representatives etc – are in a vast reception room. Refreshments are laid out at one side, under cellophane wrapping that many are tempted to breach, especially those of us who had neglected to take breakfast into account before leaving home at 4.30 am. Nobody suits the action to the wish.

General discussion rolls forward, mainly to do with the prospects and pitfalls facing the Eastern Cape. Then attendants shuffle people aside so as to partition the room with a vast pair of regal double doors. Raymond takes Jay and his staff to the side where the eats are. The rest of us spend the best part of an hour awaiting our betters' return. In the course of it a young woman from a Port Elizabeth newspaper asks for a glass of water and is told: sorry, the cups and glasses are on the other side.

Between recurring bouts of the question '*this* is democracy?' I am fascinated by the double doors. These, in scale if not trimmings, could have been designed for Louis XIV or Emperor Bokassa or the Sultan of Brunei, and one of them is broken, lolling squiff to its bearings with a big see-through triangle showing. Benefiting from much opportunity to contemplate this door, I arrive at a syllogistic revelation. In the South Africa I'd like best there would be no potentates. But if there were potentates they would live in human houses built on human scale. But if there were potentates living in potentate

165

houses with potentate frills, they would at least keep the things in order.

Did matters improve after we had disposed of the ceremonial? No, matters descended, from queasy querying into nightmare.

For two days, we drove. The idea was for the national minister and the provincial premier to butter up the Transkei. The Transkei was getting twitchy about alleged Hharabe — ie Ciskei side — domination of Eastern Cape affairs.* Jay 'n Ray would do the whistle-stop, shake hands, kiss babies, smile benignly, and remotivate, in case the twitchiness led to serious undesirability such as votes for the PAC.

Unfortunately the drawing of the schedule had evidently mistaken our parade of Toyotas and Nissans for a Formula One rally and the Transkei's livestock-strewn byways for autobahns.

So we drove, and enjoyed among other things the novel sensation of moving at three times the legal speed limit. I speak as one who can find it in his heart to confess he has been known, perhaps even more than once, to break a speed limit. It is rare, however, that I would double the limit, and to treble it is something else again.

The trebling was in 60k areas, which usually meant you were on dirt roads to start with and were going through repair works. Our drivers tended towards a macho interpretation of following distance, viz the length of a fishing rod. Frequently we could see nothing but the tail lights of the car in front.

My status being indistinct (not to say a protocol officer's nightmare, one of the small joys of my irregular profession), I spent half the time driving with Jay in a new Maxima's airconned armrest splendour, and the other half squashed with

* The prime reason that the Eastern Cape has now followed the fashion of abolishing the old district number-plates — CB, CF, CAD etc — and is making the expensive switch to boring and unnecessary provincial plates, is closely related. It is so that Gcalekas in their XA cars do not attract adverse attention in Mdantsane and vice versa.

the journos into a press combi which I take to have been Dr Porsche's prototype. Which of these means of conveyance was the less appetising is hard to say.

Not that the company was in any way defective — far from it. With Jay I discussed politics and economics and their adjuncts in the way you never normally have the time or the intimacy to do properly. Jokes and reminiscence were not absent either and generally Jay was a perfect travelling companion. The journos in the combi — all locals apart from us — were a lively and lekker bunch and there we batted at the same issues on a different level of abstraction, with less decorum. The social environment was fine. The problem was a matter of motion.

Jay's exec saloon was happily one of these newfangled ones (at least by my standards; I've had one car less than ten years old, and it was eight) which have belts in the back seats. But Jay's driver, an amiable Afrikaner who had joined up under the Verwoerd administration, made up for that.

While Jay and I debated the State of the Nation, the flow was regularly interrupted by strangulated breath-holdings. Shapes and figures, human, animal, or vegetable in the form of trees, appeared and disappeared like ghostly visions in a dust storm raised by the police car in front. One open-mouthed old man will live with me forever, and I suspect with Jay too. His jaw hung to his collarbone. He loomed for a split second in the dust, choked and pebble-spattered. Our wing mirror must have missed his chest by millimetres. There were another six equally blind cars to come. If he survived both collision and heart attack I bet he'll never again stray more than two metres from his fireplace as long as he lives.

Another old man was tottering into Umtata in an ancient bakkie held together by wire and laden with agriculture, and failed to promptly vacate the seigneurial path. The police in the two front cars leaned gravity-defying out of their windows, screeching and shaking fists and brandishing guns. Since the cars were unmarked and the police in plain-clothes and their communication at 100-plus decibels, he might have found it challenging to gather the gist of their message. I suspect he thought they were hoodlums. Whatever he thought, he drove his dilapidated truck into a ditch. As we sped past he was grinding to a diagonal halt with his bodywork peeling off behind him and his wares strewing across the ground.

The combi offered a varied brand of adrenalin flow. It was incapable of keeping up with the procession, despite the driver's best endeavours, and its pace per se was relatively gentle on the pulse. On the other hand, it lacked stopping power. Combi brakes are worrisome at the best of times, overfilled combis more so, and overfilled out-of-condition combis with smooth tyres on wet roads most of all. We'd hit up to about 140 on downhills while I prayed that the passing cattle would pay due care to the road rules. That many of their breed had neglected to do so was patent from the carcasses and skeletons we passed. Moreover the combi's wipers didn't work, which enhanced the drama as the rain was doing its civic duty assiduously. The leftmost of the four front-seat passengers operated the wipers by hand with an ingenious wire contraption which meant that he got soaked and everybody else got sprayed and we had about 5% visibility, which is fivefold more than we had while he had to pause in moments of fatigue.

If the travelling was not wholly edifying, neither were the pauses. The term 'whistle-stop' is deceptively leisurely. This was laser-stop. Lusikisiki, Port St Johns, Mount Ayliff, Mount Frere, Bizana . . . We touched down at each and having touched, untouched. Messrs Naidoo and Mhlaba would tumble out, rush headlong through a supposedly inspiring address to such of the locpops as could be mustered (we ranged between one hour and five hours late), and pile back in for the next round of dodgem cars.

At Peelton we were met by a hundred or so people, of whom 45% were under 18 and 45% over 65. After the speeches a beautiful schoolgirl with a million-dollar voice led the singing of Nkosi Sikelele. That is, she got through those two words, with the crowd beginning to join in, when the mayor loudly squelched the anthem on the grounds that the dignitaries were hasty. The schoolgirl burst into tears.

At Bizana the speechifying was in a pitch-dark tent and was punctuated by the sound system zooming with metronomic regularity from nil to max and back. Not quite *at* the point of a gun, but close, the guests of honour were press-ganged into visiting the hospital. That visit consisted of walking into one ward, uttering pleasantries, and walking out, which left the hospital mense in a state of shock, but nothing like the shock of the school headmaster who waited inside his gates to greet us formally. The procession stopped, the main ouens alighted, waved, nodded understandingly, got right back in their cars, and departed, leaving the headmaster standing with hand outstretched in unrequited greeting and feeling like he'd been slapped with a wet fish. Also, leaving yours faithfully Charlie Chump standing beside him watching my ticket to civilisation vanish into the hills.

Bit of a funny feeling, gazing down the main street of a Third World dorp with not a jacket round your shoulders nor a coin in your pocket. Jay had figured I was with the combi and Andy & Co that I was with Jay, but not far out of town Louis wondered why my jacket was in the combi and a local journo recollected that I'd been standing at the school after Jay's car left, and they came back, the good and decent people. Meantime the school-master seemed to think I must be somebody important – a mistake often made to strangers bearing white skins in places where a white skin is a rare commodity – and regaled me with the weighty amalgam of triumph and woe that he had prepared for the bigshots. It boiled down to that he had achieved X% exemptions and Y% passes despite having no teachers, no books, no paper, and no rooms.

I loved that Bizana schoolmaster. He was so determined and he was trying so hard and even though his wail was utterly justified he wasn't letting it get on top of him. Individually and severally I loved plenty of people we met in the Transkei. Jointly and collectively the place was a dreadful decrepit wasteland. For one thing, outside Umtata there are almost no phones. If the wires haven't been stolen the exchanges have collapsed. Usually both, I gather. Transkei landscape is marked by four central features: spectacular natural majesty, crashed cars, the corpses of crashed-into cattle, and leaning telephone poles with their wires cut off. Why they're leaning, heaven knows, but lean they do and there are places where you can see an entire mosaic of poles leaning every whichway, a crazy paving each with four little quarter-metre stretches of forlorn line dangling in the wind to remind you that in some previous epoch every pole was connected to its neighbours either side.

There are no cellphone masts whatsoever, a phenomenon for which everybody has some complicated conspiratorial explanation. In many places there is no post either, the post offices having ceased to function. If you wish to tell your grandma in Cofimvaba that you got engaged, divorced, a child, a job, a suspended sentence, or a parliamentary seat, you pitch up in person in the fashion of your forefathers. You make like babamkhulumkhulu did before the wicked colonialists introduced odious foreign practices such as mail, addresses and electricity.

Communications hiatus aside, there's omnipresent decay. The old colonial dorpies feel like Kolmanskop, the Namib ghost town that you come across periodically in calendars and waiting room magazines, with sand flowing through the once grandiose portals. The Transkei dorpies are short of sand and their portals were merely bourgeois, but to look at them is to think of Kolmanskop. Decay is in the nostrils, the eyeballs, the ears and the soul.

Port St Johns is in as beautiful a corner of the earth as anyone ever saw, and was once a thriving dorp. Now the various ex-hotels are burnt down or closed, except for a lonely bar that sustains an incongruously vigorous night-life in one small portion of an otherwise dark and grim edifice. The shops are gone, the streets are ruined, the floorboards of the town hall are like a choppy sea.

Butterworth, the second biggest Transkei town, would be a strong bet if there was a competition for World's Dirtiest Municipality. Arriving for our meeting there we circum-navigated rubbish mounds as if we were in a slalom laid on by the Institute for Advanced Motoring. We were ushered into the town hall to be met by a squeezed ululating mass of thousands of ANCniks, and for the first time and I deeply trust the last as well I was pushed onto the stage at a party political rally. The lights kept dimming and resurging, as if an exhausted person was grinding a generator by hand with a slavemaster administering intermittent invigoratory lashes.

All this was perverse. When I was a kid Port St Johns was idyllic and Butterworth was tidy and illuminated and vorentoe, and both places upset me because they closed their doors against the common people. Now the doors are as open as Boeing hangars, and both places upset me because they're disasters.

As to *why* they are disasters... well, Jay knew. Everywhere we went, he explained that the RDP couldn't deliver overnight 'because we are fighting the legacy of 40 years of apartheid; we are fighting the legacy of 300 years of white rule'. This line went down well. One place Jay stated it was the Lusikisiki town hall, to which the legacy of apartheid had bequeathed a public toilet system which I visited with an intent that turned to merciful constipation when I beheld the filth on display. Others had been less squeamish. Copious use had been made of the floor, with what effect upon the shoes of the later-comers I did not wish to dwell upon, and the level of faeces and torn newspaper in the bowl was higher than the rim — a sight that posed a remarkable anatomical riddle which I for one am willing to let remain unsolved.

The permeating decay became a central if unresolved part of the colloquy in the back of Jay's car. His arguments were that (a) the old government had neglected Transkei disgracefully and (b) when people have absolutely nothing that includes absolutely no bootstraps with which to pull themselves up. I don't dispute the neglect factor and in principle I am deeply sympathetic with the bootstraps factor, but I'm no longer swallowing these as a whole answer or even a major part. Apartheid didn't smother that town hall toilet with shit. And which legacy of white rule was holding back Jay's delivery? The newspapers that clogged the sewers? The cistern? The flushing water? The bricks that encased the place? The nails, the screws, the timber, the door, the hinges, the plaster?

Jay's message, as I heard it over and over, came across to me as 'the whites screwed you terribly, but stick around because when we get into gear we'll sort you out'. Jay said no, he was exhorting the people to pull finger and join partnerships with the government. I had to feel it was a subtle exhortation.

I didn't object to Jay's politicking. That was fair enough. What worried me was the insistent echo of a common problem. Too many people are spending too much of their headspace believing that somebody else is going to solve their problems. At this rate the Port St Johns town hall will end up with no floorboards at all.

I came away with in many ways a renewed respect for Jay. He had been astoundingly willing to stand his ground in the two on-camera confrontations I had with him, and in each he gave at least as good as he got. A lesser minister would have ducked, resorting to time pressures or any of the many easy subterfuges available to the guy who is handing the orders around. I know that many a minister would, after the first interview which was a definite departure from the Ja-Baas norm, have made damn sure to duck the second. Not Jay. I also acquired a vastly fuller appreciation of why the RDP mattered than I had had before, which is also a vastly fuller appreciation than the average citizen has ever had.

The RDP was not just a Father Christmas in the business of 'releasing' a billion rand here or a million rand there, as its public image became. It was meant to be a genuinely grand plan to marshal the energies of State in the service of progress. That it conked was not least because of the immense difficulty of securing headlines and attention for anything beyond the simplistic numbers game. Its ambition and its potential was far larger than South Africa now will ever know. Finally I suppose you have to blame Jay and his department for failing to grip the public imagination as it deserved to be gripped, but what the RDP deserved is real nonetheless. I find myself – not for the first time in a disregarded minority – profoundly regretful that the government chickened out of it.

The Transkei Trek reawakened my appreciation for Jay and the RDP (and Trekwise it provided our own little moment of history in the form of the longest single sequence we have ever broadcast – an uninterrupted 14-minute discussion between myself and Jay on a hill above the Holiday Inn overlooking Umtata). But it also shivered my timbers in respect of the running of Africa.

South Africa's challenge is to get the democratic whole working in the way that the formerly white parts are used to. South Africa's threat is that the democratic whole ends up working in the way that the formerly black parts have become increasingly used to. I would like the sewers of Lusikisiki and the telephones of Cofimvaba to operate like the sewers of Johannesburg and the telephones of Bloemfontein, or for that matter of Pilgrim's Rest or Haga Haga or Philippolis or any of thousands of white dorps. I have a fear of the movement of the future becoming a movement in the opposite direction.

12
Armada

I've been giving you a whack of the philosophising and the agonising and the questioning and the What It All Means. Maybe you'd like some straightforward highlight experiences. In one way that would be difficult, as there were highlights in every Trek, even in the ten or twelve where I actively disliked the final product. But over the next few chapters I'd like to offer a sampling, and for no particular reason I begin in Lesotho.

We went to Lesotho with the police stock theft unit. For them it's an annual outing. Every winter Mother Nature lowers the grazing altitude and thereby limits the range of hideouts available to an ill-gotten herd. And in deep midwinter the stock theft unit occupies northern Lesotho. In 1995 we were part of the occupation, not wholly comfortably.

My mental picture of the stock theft function envisaged the arm of the white man's law reaching across the Caledon to grip the throat of the penniless black neighbour state and rub its nose in the

hollowness of its independence. On behalf of the Mercedes-driving Free State farmer we were to terrorise the peasantry and punish the barely eating Sotho rustler. I couldn't fault the legality and even the major part of the morality. If I had sukkeled to husband my herd and feed my land and balance my books I would clamour as loud as the next man for the SAP to thump the guy who cut my fence and drove my prize cattle across the river bed. But at the same time... discomfort happened. As we began, I felt like part of an invading army, stripping their all from those who had little so those who had plenty could have a bit more.

The stock theft manne, and especially the admirable Sergeant Niemand who was our principal escort, laboured nobly to disabuse me.

'It's not like that,' said Niemand. 'There's no terrorising at all, more of a ritual festival really, and about 90% of the cattle we recover belong to the Basotho anyway.'

Tell it to the marines, I thought.

Yeah well. A prejudice has no better corrective than experience.

The night before the round-up was party night. We had a huge encampment in the mountains a long way from any known dot on the map. Four gigantic campfires were on the go when our police 4x4 pulled in at dusk: one for the white SAPs, one for the black SAPs, one for the Royal Lesotho Police, one for the complainants. With the exception of the Lesotho colonel in charge, who divided his time between the Lesotho fire and the white one, the separate groups might as well have been divided by concrete walls.

My love-and-brotherhood instincts rebelled at the division — dashit, weren't we all colleagues in a joint quest — so I tried my hand at a bit of undividing, and failed. Each of the three black camps was less than delighted by Andrew Grealy's sun-gun, the zillion-watt spotlight that dazzled whoever I was talking to. When I tried the brotherhood bit on my own it was no better.

The same three camps were uncomfortable at my mere white presence. They wanted to talk home-talk in home language and make the most of the free beer. The last thing they needed was some freelance anti-apartheid missionary poking about into their off-duty. Funny thing, when you think of it: the rainbow is not after all an amalgam of the colours, it's the diametric opposite.

The Boere's fire was eminently convivial. The Lesotho colonel's frequent pit-stops were received each time with great fanfare and welcome. The two black members of our crew were also fully embraced as participants, and the process notched up another ratchet on the endless learning curve of understanding South Africa. Ten or twenty years ago our men and the Lesotho colonel would also have been siphoned off into an ethnic corner. Next year the colonel's two supporting majors may also cross the divides. In some unspecifiable time to come black SAP officers and then NCOs will eat at the whiteys' fire and, not tomorrow or even the day after but someday, the SAP's two fires will shrink to one. Change does take place, but not at the pace that the media discourse and those who fit in it tend to think.

We'd been told how to sleep — head in a balaclava, tomorrow's clothes laid out under your body or they'd be frozen by morning. Two hours before dawn, the armada rolled.

The stock theft drivers do not lose sleep over the longevity of their tyres, springs, shock absorbers, engines, or teeth fillings. Even so, if Bruce Fordyce had been racing us to penetrate the valley earmarked to host the morning fun, our convoy would have come a poor second. This place was not designed for vehicular traffic.

Policepersons in general consider the use of seatbelts to be unmanly. The stock theft ouens evidently consider it impermissible to even have an intact usable seatbelt in your vehicle. This made for an interesting ride. The driver has his wheel for balance; passengers use their limbs as stanchions. For the unpractised this results in the novel sensation of emerging from a 60km motorised trip with exhausted muscles. You're going to be stiff for days. Several times our vehicle tilted to such crazy angles that I thought 'this is it, this is where we roll'. We never did.

By the end we'd covered two large valleys, on opposite sides of the same mountain. It had taken four bone-rattling hours to get from Valley A to Valley B. We went back by helicopter, and passed over Valley A in 3 minutes 20 seconds.

The round-up itself was a picnic, in more ways than one. The choppers dropped us on selected peaks in sticks of (usually) three people, and we ambled down. The most fearsome weapon in the SAP's possession was a walking stick. If the police advertised the function as a hiking vacation, people would pay for it. We strolled through exquisite mountain scenery, chatting relaxedly of ships and shoes and sealing wax and stock.

The manne had a large number of regimental legends. Many of these were to do with the startlingly numerous and violent cattle wars which are evidently on the go all the time both inside Lesotho and on its Free State and Transkei borders. Entirely unfazed, in the way one may recount a round of golf, they told yesterday stories and last-week stories that belong in the Middle Ages, involving the razing of villages, burning of babies, wholesale pillage and other deterrents against renewed cattle theft or suspected theft. They gave me a wholly new comprehension of the ferocities that cattle theft creates, particularly when the parties are neighbouring villages. It was a medieval picture mingled with High Noon and Dodge City, with themselves as so many sheriffs and the media-consuming public enlightened to the extent of three paragraphs on page 23. Times like this, the magnitude of what we don't know about what's happening seems overwhelming.

The other top topic is the unit's tracking prowess. Their greatest pride is a colleague, a constable despite 30 years in the unit (and a pale complexion), who would leave base alone on horseback with a rucksack of rations and return four months later beladen with gifts from Sotho chiefs and with dozens of stolen cattle accompanying him.

A career in stock theft, they loved to say, required a special breed. I could believe that all right. Also that a bit of third-degree interrogation amid the mountain-tops would never echo as far as the courthouses of the rulebound world below. But whatever might happen unseen and unheard, the bit that I saw was what Niemand had said, a festival.

The choppers' roar had told everybody what was coming. But the convention seemed to be, do nothing until it came. So as we walked down the mountain, in the demeanour and the clothing of holiday hikers, the people mobilised. They greeted the police; the police greeted them; never once in my sight did anyone need to be told what to do; they rounded up their cattle and sheep and drove them down in vague parallel with us. The further we went the bigger the caravan grew until by the end I felt like an extra in a Ben Hur refugee scene, surrounded by hooves and breathing more dust than oxygen.

The armada was drawn up at a central plain. Perhaps five thousand animals were corralled into a wedge-shaped man-made corridor. At the thin end of the wedge claimants laid their claims, with the Sotho police — SA Sotho and Lesotho Sotho jointly — arbitrating off the cuff.

In theory the deciding factor was the brandmark. In practice the brandmark was mainly a joke. It was usually on the animal's ears, but only about a third of the animals still possessed two ears. That one (or both) had been cut off was a surefire giveaway that the animal had been stolen somewhere along the way, but pointed only the shakiest of suspicious fingers at the current possessor. It might easily have been lawfully bought by him after a previous recovery. It might well have been stolen from him himself, and recovered.

Even where the marks were on less dispensable portions of the anatomy, they meant little. The police pointed out Bs that had turned to 8s or vice versa, Zs to 2s, Cs to Os and so on.

Largely, the police looked at the relationship between claimant and cow. In some cases this relationship was a dead cert. There was an old man with Parkinson's disease whose cattle behaved like dogs towards him, licking and slurping and nuzzling for their tummies to be scratched. One cow was only happy when its head was resting on his shoulder. There was no question about these cattle. When he was reunited with them the crowd cheered.

The rights and wrongs were rarely that obvious. At peak there were perhaps two hundred claimants present, and about double that locals. If an allocation evoked a major grumble from either side, the police would call the winner back and run an appeal hearing, which did not always result in a reversed judgment. Mostly, the division of spoils was extremely speedy and generally approved.

A nice feature of the affair was that for once the black police were wholly in charge – a radical contrast from the dispensation in all other matters, where the only black person who ever said as much as boo to a goose was the colonel, and even he didn't push it any further than that. He was treated very respectfully but as a kind of guest-of-honour. In command terms the shots were called by a youthful white lieutenant, to whom the colonel seemed happy to defer. At times while the armada was rrarh-rrarh-rrarhing through the countryside with the choppers choppa-choppa-chopping overhead and the only forms of order we encountered were occasional schools and spaza shops, I could not get rid of the melodramatic impression that our 25-year-old host was for the time being the de facto military dictator of northern Lesotho.

The other feature of the judging process was espionage. The place appeared to be riddled with informers, who played a clouded role in the stock search but a clear role in a dagga bust. Somebody reported a dagga grower. The police scrambled. The suspect was but half a kilometre from us by tape-measure, but it was a 5K road trip. Bizarrely, we could watch two

179

simultaneous scenes all the way. We watched the 4x4s negotiating the road while we watched the mounting agitation at the target homestead.

I got there during the mop-up. The main man was under a relaxed form of guard, with friends coming to bid what everybody evidently knew was going to be a long farewell. The police were piling bale upon bale into Landrovers. It struck me that if the historical cookie had crumbled the opposite way there could have been power round-ups of whiskey and wine, with the law enforcers going home to enjoy a relaxing weed after a hard day's work.

Back at the corral a few hundred head of livestock had been liberated to claimants who were then and there starting to shepherd them back to the four corners of Lesotho. One guy I spoke to was from Morija way down south. He had been granted two sheep, with which he was happily embarking on several days' walk home.

Another forty-odd head, mainly cattle, were loaded onto trucks for return to commercial farmers across the border. All of these cattle were accompanied by bedraggled herdsmen. Whereas the police did not in general offer much in the way of a philosophical rationale of the proceedings, they had a common and fierce view of the role of these employed herdsmen, namely that it was disgusting. Separately and at different times a dozen or more Afrikaner cops whispered to me that the treatment of the herdsmen was an unrecognised scandal. These people, they said, were sent to follow round-ups for weeks at a time, and given sums of ten or twenty rands to live on. The police were not impressed with the employment practices of their landed kinsmen.

Generally, too, the expedition was devoid of political talk or indeed of any recognition of politics whatsoever. However, at the end of our time in the second valley, which was the more spectacular but also by far the harder to reach, a fellow with a good deal of English (most people had none at all) and a fair amount of Marxist theory buttonholed me. He let fly with an angry perspective on oppression. The people of this valley, he said, had nothing. They were forced to spend their lives toiling underground on my mines so that I, the white South African, could live like a king.

I said that my sympathy for this predicament was muted. Tens of thousands of people populated this valley, yet they had never got their joint act together even to the extent of beating out a rudimentary access road such as sheer manpower could have done any time since the advent of the iron age. I was not about to catch the Guilt virus because they didn't have washing machines or microwaves.

We agreed to disagree.

13

Blame it on the Darkies

When we wanted a programme on Affirmative Action, it seemed all wrong to do it the normal way. Look at us: Beckett, Burnett, Davidson, Grealey, Ingham, Laudati, Lee, Marsh, Modena, Reilly, Shaw, Stilwell. The editors and directors and producers and managers of the Trek were male to a man, pale ditto, and packed Anglo-Saxon. That list could have been the Hilton College Fourth XI, 1923. Michael Modena and Dante Laudati obligingly possessed Italian grandfathers which brought the only smack of cultural diversity to the decision-making process, and that was a smack that hasn't mattered since the 18th century. We were too monochrome for comfort, and for this programme at least I wanted a real, full, indigenous presence.

My old friend and one-time employee Duma Ndlovu, returned from twenty years' exile, was making movies. I stiffened the sinews and asked Keith & Co to kindly bow out for the occasion. This was an irregular thing to do. One does not normally say to an established partner: sorry, but just this once I want somebody else, and then I'll come back to you. It's not all that far removed from saying to a spouse: sorry, but just tonight I want someone else, and then I'll come back to you. I considered it a hard proposition to put to Keith, and was well prepared with explanations and justifications.

Keith cut me short. 'Fine,' he said. 'I supppose Duma will need our facilities.'

This was generous, all right. To be true, it was not generosity alone, as this way Keith would at least charge out on the hi-tech equipment which was now largely devoted to the Trek and whose every unutilised moment cost arms and legs. But he could, and many would, have resented the relegation. His calm acquiescence was real magnanimity.

Duma had difficulties of his own about benefiting from an affirmative action job and being thereby made to feel like a charity case. He needed the work, all right, but he would have preferred to get work from his skills than from his complexion.

We talked it through and agreed that, as he said, while it might not be ideal it would be ridiculous to say no.

The start was not propitious. Armed with Keith's cameras and Keith's lights and Keith's microphones and borne by Keith's combi (in the hands of Keith's regular driver, Joe Dlamini), we set forth to our first appointment. It fell through. We proceeded to our second appointment. It fell through. Early now for our next appointment, we paused at a park in, of all places, stable non-affirmative Houghton. While the camera watched, Duma and I shared a park bench and had a harsh verbal fight about Affirmative Action and affiliated subjects, and thereby put our first short slice of footage onto tape. We got back to the road. The combi had been stolen.

The combi had put thousands of hours and multiple thousands of kilometres into the service of the Trek, all of them in the hands of Shaw Pictures. The worst that had befallen it was a window mechanism going wonky. In half a morning in the hands of the Affirmative replacements, without setting tread beyond our own back yard, it became the ex-combi.

It was horribly obvious what everybody was thinking. Duma and his eloquent Africanist cameraman Sanku were the only ones to put it into words: 'Howcome as soon as we darkies are involved, something goes wrong?'

There was no answer to that one. Duma's team could not in any possible way whatsoever be blamed for Fate having chosen that day to redistribute the combi. Nor — contrary to easy imagination — did the two missed appointments have anything to do with dud arrangements or dud timekeeping or any other ready-made stereotype. They were two of the justifiable mishaps that occur occasionally to even the most Teutonic arrangements and just happened, on this day, to occur in freak succession. It also just happened on the same shoot that:

(a) a tape got lost;

(b) another tape was defective, with that malicious kind of defect that you only discover *after* it has been fully used;

(c) the camera broke.

All this was awesomely instructive in a most disconcerting way. Duma, like every black entrepreneur I know, is convinced that the cards are stacked against black business. It seemed as if a supernatural power was bent on proving him right.

Had I not been on the spot throughout, and had Duma after the event outlined this litany of curious cosmic sabotage, I would have had to think: 'See what happens when you get the blacks in.' As it is, I knew beyond trace of doubt that there was no such connection. Logically, a string of chance events should have no meaning whatsoever. Coincidence is coincidence. Illogically, it left me with more sympathy than previously for the complaint about the stacking of the cards.

Then again, the cards at Pepsi were stacked okay. Pepsi's head office is in shouting distance of the scene of the ex-combi's last stand. Combiless, we made our way there, and not for the first time it struck me as a pity that the growth of black business takes place in the whitest possible vicinities.

This cookie could easily have crumbled the other way. It could have become the fashion for the upcoming spearheads of black empowerment to base themselves in the townships. The *coulds* are exciting. Imagine Soweto as a real city, with the Nails and Rails and Kagisos and Thebes and Pepsis and Vivos powering the way to a first-world commercial hub right there among their people. Imagine other, not necessarily 'Black', firms following in their wake, bringing meaningful retailing and significant service to the townships, with malls and cinemas and order. Imagine an organised and forceful presence in Soweto, putting vigour into sorting out the place's policing and robot-repair and road-rules and sightliness.

Ah, dreamland. What we actually have is a ghetto, which in a major way has been cursed more than blessed by the ending of apartheid. Back then, the townships with all their problems at least enjoyed the unquestioning loyalty of the mover-and-shaker echelon of black society. Now they are increasingly left to the no-hopers. Everybody who can get out, gets out. Residentially, the middle-class bits that were status in the '80s are now apologetic staging-posts on the route to Kelvin or Buccleuch. Commercially, no heavyweight black business would be seen dead with a Soweto address. Even a town address means also-ran. *Aiysh, town's so black now, y'know.* It's Sandton, man, that's the place to be, Sandton or a larnie Houghton office park with fountains, which is where we spoke to Khehla Mthembu.

Khehla, transmogrified from old-style firebrand Azapo president to new-style suave chairman of Pepsi, still with the same daunting bench-press build and the same vastly engaging good humour, is a prime example of what Affirmative Action ought to mean. This is no token chairman, shoved into a big office to make the letterhead look nice. He's real, real, real. He wasn't buying any little portion of my proposition that the unreal bulk of the Affirmative Action business was vitiating the whole purpose. No black businessman is buying that proposition yet, at least not on camera, but with Khehla the debate was real and I was delighted to screen it − not least the parts where I came off the most sorrily second − as a corrective to sceptical whites who too easily dismiss *all* black executive pioneering as just another Affirmative Action token.

Duma's schedule took several further twists and turns, one of them, rather marvellously, to a paraffin-lit hostel dormitory in which a plot was being hatched to buy one of the country's bluest-chip finance houses. The whole process, though, was underlain by a consistent toothachy sense of having betrayed the loan of the combi.

We did what we could about the combi in every way, from nagging the police to broadcasting appeals on Radio 702 to conducting our own sleuthing.

Finally we got a lead, an address in Alexandra. A posse squashed into Duma's BMW, squeezed like students trying for a Guinness record. Discussion arose as to the correct form of approach. I was for innocently knocking on the door and saying 'Excuse me but if anybody happens to come across a green combi SZP 966T we'd be happy to offer a couple of thousand rand and ask no questions.' I was outvoted, not to say howled down, as hopelessly naive. Everybody else being black, and this being their territory, as it were, I bowed to the protests and we made for the Alex police station. After much initial suspicion, the police entered the spirit of things with a vengeance. We proceeded to the tipped address in 8th Street − one of the formerly gracious Alex homes with stoep and garden and elegance, now a shack settlement − with a platoon of heavily armed lawmen in tow.

At my insistence the police stayed well to the rear. This was not through any wish to be Wyatt Earp, but for precisely the opposite reason. I am terrified of guns at the best of times, and doubly terrified when two sides of a potential conflict both have fingers on triggers. If we all pulled up together, police alighting with firepower in hand, somebody who might have something on his conscience might just take fright and do something rash. I calculated that to have a barmy unarmed longhaired whitey politely asking after a stray vehicle would be less likely to awaken worries. At the same time, if anybody did happen to experience worries, the sight of the artillery up the road would help deter certain forms of expression of such worries.

So I tried my if-you-please trick and got nowhere. There were maybe thirty people on the premises and well, waddayaknow, half of them happened to be working on combis. Everybody evidently had a funny eyesight problem. They could see their nuts and bolts and screws but couldn't see me. Hearing, too. I couldn't escape the memory of that schoolboy phrase 'lost fart in a thunderstorm' which summed up my perceptions as I wandered about trying to get a response.

When the law of diminishing returns reached terminal, I made a short rueful observation to the camera and turned to leave. Duma, however, had his head in a combi engine, which he appeared to be studying in intimate detail in the company of two other buried heads. I didn't suppose he was providing technical advice.

Adjudging it inappropriate to initiate a discussion about the political economy of Alexandra, I stretched my arms, and twiddled my thumbs, and savoured the sunshine, and cooled my heels, and looked insouciant, and whistled a happy tune, and then another happy tune, and then another, and another, and started to wonder what was for supper, until finally Duma's mechanical inspection came to an abrupt end and he hustled me out of the place without a rearward glance.

In the car, Duma said: 'He was telling me that if we hadn't been such fools as to come with a white man and a camera and the police they might have had more to say to us.'

I said: 'Does that mean you can go back later?'

Duma said: 'No, they were getting threatening. They wouldn't listen to my excuses.'

'What were your excuses?'

'I said: "Man, you know these whites. It's that mlungu who brought the police, don't hold it against me".'

Well, there's the most instant answer I ever heard to any whitey who suffers agonies of doubt about whether the white man has a role in Africa. Relax, friend, you're needed. If nothing else, you're needed for permanent excuse.

Slightly shaken by the concatenation of events, Duma and I occupied the back of the BM. While Joe chauffeured, Sanku contorted himself into an impossible position facing backward from the front. With his feet doubled under his buttocks and the dashboard thrusting brutally into his back, a stance that would have half the world's video cameramen shrieking for their shop steward, Sanku rolled that fat unwieldy camera for an hour while Duma and I scoured the streets of Alex for green combis and simultaneously resumed our earlier argument.

This was cheat footage, in its way. Since when are you allowed to make a TV programme out of a wrangle between producer and presenter? But we shot it anyway, thinking that out of it would come a minute or so to wrap the programme up.

When we went through the tape, one feature became extremely evident: Duma's fights with me were where it came alive. There were several nice bits in the 'real' interviews, but there was also one lo-o-o-ng load of platitude mouthing. Nearly all Affirmative talk, after all, consists of the same set of well worn clichés being re-stated in different order and different inflection.

Here was something else. I was saying that Affirmative Action had become a pathetic distortion which consisted of appointing the wrong people to the wrong jobs for the wrong reasons. Duma was saying that was probably true, but the alternative was to leave the whites full of odious superiority, which was worse. I said that if your aim was to entrench the odious superiority you couldn't do better than keep shovelling blacks into jobs on the far side of their vuurmaakplek. Duma said at least some of those guys rose to vuurmaakpleks you had never expected of them. With that I could agree.

Neither of us were greatly satisfied with either that discussion or where the programme had gone on the whole, but then, we'd been there. It's never the same to people who hadn't been there.

In this case the people who hadn't been there were the entire human race minus four; except it wasn't really four because Joe was negotiating the roads of Alex, a slalom between taxis and pedestrians and goats, and therefore was in no position to concentrate on the words of wisdom emanating from behind, and Sanku was trying to keep his back from breaking and his camera from shaking and therefore ditto. So the entire human race minus two were in a position to see the unedited footage and make comments uncluttered by the nuances of what was not on camera.

The percentage of candidates who availed themselves of this opportunity was modest, but the comment which arose was unanimous: the argument in the BMW made the show. So, allowed or not allowed, the programme after umpteen hours of formal researched interviews and exhausting travelling con-sisted largely of an in-house squabble which you might have taken for the work of forty minutes.

The effect was nowhere near the same league numerically as the Rave or the hijackers or the taxi war, but for those who like this kind of thing, well, they liked this kind of thing. A batch of reviews in diverse newspapers, most notably Maureen Barnes in the Cape Times, said that an actual nitty-gritty on this holy cow subject was rare and welcome. The views of the critics, as is well known, have nil in common with the views of the punters (or why does the much-lauded McKellen adaptation of Richard III play to half-houses while the derided Lipstiek Dipstiek makes a fortune) but they do on the whole reflect the perspective of the discerning minority, and I am not among those TV performers who claim to be impervious to them.

The Trek had enjoyed pretty good treatment at the hands of the critics — even from Robert Kirby, whose mercurial pen is more comfortable in vitriol than in ink (and who ruined a long-awaited family holiday with a review of my first book; I spent the week in Machadodorp wondering if I could ever be seen in public again). Kirby must have had an off day when he got around to the Trek, as he was positively polite about it. Others had been civil too, and sometimes enlightening. Michele Witthaus in Business Day, for instance, offered the world an inspired exposition on how my track record of independence had earned me the right to stand up on TV and say anything I like. Let alone that I loved that 'earned', Michele's explanation of what we were doing explained things to me as much as to the uninvolved reader.

The reviews had been mainly non-brutal, but Duma's programme tugged a particular switch. Straight talk about Affirmative Action!? That was news. Like snow. In December.

Duma's confidence was wobbly by the time we delivered to Auckland Park. Maureen Barnes, and the other critics who were generally less full-frontal, did wonders to restore it.

Question: Does Duma now get regular non-affirmative TV work?

Answer: May we please move on to the next question?

14

Amabokoboko

South Africa is commonly called a 'rugby-mad country'. Properly considered, it is nothing of the sort.

The population is divided into two categories, being:

(1) Rugby Fans, and

(2) Non-Fans.

Non-Fans are divided into two sub-categories:

(i) Feigned Fans or FFs, and

(ii) Couldn't Care a Continentals, or CCCs.

FFs *pretend* to take an interest, for reasons such as not to come across as nerds (male) or not to disappoint their spouses (female). CCCs do not pretend to take an interest. To them it is a matter of sublime indifference who kicks more balls than who else, not to mention who gouges more heads, bites more ears, rakes more calves, bloodies more noses or blackens more eyes.

As is clear from the following scientific survey results, Fans are outnumbered from backside to breakfast time by Non-Fans.

	FANS	NON-FANS	
		FFs	CCCs
Males			
African	10 000	0	19 990 000
Coloured	100 000	1 000	1 899 000
Indian	50 000	500	949 500
White	2 000 000	499 998	2
Females			
African	0	0	20 000 000
Coloured	0	100	1 999 900
Indian	0	50	999 950
White	2	2 000 000	499 998

Total Fans: 2 160 002   Total Non-Fans: 47 839 998

Unfortunately, proving that the world is an unjust place, the 47 839 998 have nil journalistic representation. Rugby matches are entirely covered by people who know a free kick from a scrum down and an off side from a knock on and who can get seriously excited by the little computer graphs showing which team has had how much possession of the ball.

This blatant obstruction of democracy is obviously something for the Constitutional Court to look into. Plus, the above objective figures show that a Commission of Inquiry must be urgently appointed under the Trade Description Act to counteract mis-descriptions such as 'rugby-mad country'.

Meantime it struck the mighty minds who organise the Trek that they possessed a rare property in the person of one of the two pale male Seffricans who couldn't give a continental about rugby or all its works, and I was press-ganged into doing a programme on the World Cup through the eyes of a Non-Fan.

This meant, inter alia, that I was supplied with a magic badge which admitted me to every game I wished to attend, thereby giving also the 2 160 002 a proof of the injustice of the human condition.

I won't say the magic badge was entirely wasted on me, as some brilliant bits of rugby did penetrate my consciousness to inspire the revelation that when rugby is brilliant it is infinitely more brilliant than breaststroke, high-jump, golf, weight-lifting, tennis, show-jumping, or anything else. But the experience did not dent my conviction that most of the time rugby is legalised barbarism, the place where you become a hero for doing things for which, if you did them elsewhere, policemen would take you away.

Moreover, I could hardly believe the crowd. If the Springboks were playing, anybody else who did anything well was booed, by a good part of the crowd. Somebody from the enemy team kicks a good kick or passes a good pass, let alone scores a good try: booooooh. The French were booed just for coming on. What's sport about that?

What, for that matter, was sport about luring makeweight teams from countries with four or six rugby clubs, like Japan and Ivory Coast, and then pounding them into dust with a cricket-score victory and calling it a world record?

Sports-wise I was not altogether converted. As a milestone on the social highway, however, the World Cup was a privilege to attend. I revelled in the novel unclutteredness of the feeling 'this is *our* team'. I rejoiced in the vibe and the spirit — make that *gees*, it doesn't bear translation even despite its extreme unphoneticism in English. I took pleasure in the spawning of a huge new breed of pavement entrepreneurs creating wealth for themselves and health for the nation. The relationships in the stands were lekker; the behaviour in the traffic jams was pleasant. People were getting on with people, feeling part of a whole; feeling a belonging.

Not least, one had to notice how the very few dark faces in the stands were received; namely, with an almost unctuous enthusiasm as if of a hotelier who frantically hopes you will come back next year and bring your friends with you. This was funny in its way, as most of the people in these crowds would not even think of attending a soccer match. It's not so much that they don't believe in *round* leather balls; many of them maintain a watching brief on Manchester United and Arsenal. It's that they don't believe in gigantic black crowds. Yet here the non-blackness of the crowd was as conspicuous as the non-blackness of the team, and not only my colour-sensitive eyes were noticing this thing. Many spectators, not necessarily consciously, would love to see a black component big enough to be comfortably NewSAn but not so big as to be uncomfortably dominant. The same sense applies to many areas of South African life, and I guess the trick is to get the mixture right. Yes, you do want to encourage blacks to feel *at home* in every portion of the land. No, you do not want non-blacks to cease to feel *at home* themselves. Quite some trick. Worth much fine-tuning.

The high point of the rugby programme was to be a private showing of Paul Slabolepszy's rugby comedy 'Heel Against the Head', in the company of the Springboks.

This seemed a pretty good deal. We'd watch the play in cosy isolation, me and my crew and the Bokke, sharing the odd laugh here and heckle there, and then afterwards we'd all go off along with Paul and his fall-guy Bill Flynn, and wrap ourselves around a convivial pasta, and the Springboks and I would have these friendly man-to-man tête-à-têtes while Richard rolled his camera.

Reality did not fulfil the script.

For a start, every alleged dignitary in Johannesburg, and his uncle, had the same impression of a personal tea-party with the Boks. The Tesson theatre was packed, and harassed ushers were tearing hair out in the attempt to sort out seating confusions.

Secondly, when the Boks arrived the last thing they wanted was an intimate chat, let alone an intimate chat with a nosy camera-bearing stranger.

I tried it anyway— hey, ain't this showbiz? Morné and Francois managed to summon up a certain pained politeness, even when I obnoxiously griped about the team's mouthsful of teeth during the singing of the Nkosi part of the anthem. The other 14 pairs of eyes were sending me the very unequivocal message that is commonly expressed by two short words, not being 'bon voyage'.

I tactically withdrew— which is to say, gave up— feeling exactly like the public's idea of the kind of journalist that you don't want your daughter to marry, a brash pushy nuisance.

The second last thing the Boks wanted was the persecution of autograph hunters. But during an event like the World Cup people get dewy about their champions and acquire a compelling need for a lock of hair, or equivalent. So the general pandemonium in the theatre was enhanced by grey-haired gentlemen and tint-rinsed ladies clambering over seats proffering programmes for the Boks to make their X.

What was worse, even the undewy tended to have children. I have three. Each had a hot favourite rugby player. Life would become fraught if I returned home without autographs. So after the excruciating experience of being invited to absent myself and my intrusive camera from the team's midst, I now had to supplement the grey-haired throng slavering for the famous signatures.

The only two Boks I could identify with confidence were Francois and Chester Williams. This was not a good time to be saying: 'Er, which one of you is James Small, please,' and what is more I got hopelessly mixed up between the Kobus Jouberts and the Andre Wieses, the Japie Strydoms and the Hannes Mulders. It took every grain of paternal affection to persevere through the embarrassment of prolonged pursuance, to say nothing of every millimetre of thick skin. In the end, of course, the delivery of the prized pieces of paper was seventh heaven for the kids, for about five minutes. By tomorrow morning they were forgotten and in the course of a spring-clean a year later I came across them in a dusty pile of old magazines.

15

Crown and Jewel

For a while in early '96, we were getting to the Oshoek border post so often that we called it Os. Swaziland came up in two successive programmes. One was on illegal immigration. We met two Ethiopians whom Divine Will had sent southwards, armed with a supply of Amharic bibles, to spread the Word. They got to Mbabane via Mozambique and paid a taxi driver R300 to take them to the SA border — a R2,50 fare for those in the know. They were promptly picked up by the SAP, and were now about to be the focus of a routine inter-governmental wrangle. Was Swaziland to carry the cost of flying them back, or was South Africa? Either way, they would just start walking south again, as they confidently assured us and their arrestors. There are not a lot more Sisyphusian jobs than Aliens Control in SA. (All right then, Sisyphus was the ou condemned forever to roll a rock up to the top of a hill from which it would keep rolling down again.)

We met one of Aliens Control's trains, too. Joburg to Maputo, every Wednesday afternoon. Front ten coaches chocabloc with illegals being repatriated. Back four coaches, a total of five paying customers between them. We ask illegals: 'Have you done this before?' Answers: 'Three times', 'five times', 'eight times'. Will they do it again? No prizes.

We also did a programme on Swaziland in its own right. Due to assorted setbacks ranging from inaudible interviews to the unfolding revolution's inconsiderate habit of outdating our material, we visited it four times. One of these delivered us an internal record of the kind that has zilch application to the benefit of mankind but that we will remember long after we have forgotten why we were there: the record for our longest ever wait for breakfast.

From the time we left Johannesburg at 4.00 am, to be at the border when it opened at dawn, we were constantly thinking: '*Just now* we'll pause for breakfast, just as soon as we have done this little thing or that little one.' But the just-nows never turned to now, and what is more it was strike day in Swaziland; we couldn't even provide interim maintenance through peanut snacks from street hawkers.

We had vowed to leave well in time for my nine o'clock Monday night radio show, but of course when we actually left it had to be broken speed limits all the way. The leaving slowed the adrenalin flow that had suppressed the stomach's complaints, so we had to pause for takeaway breakfast in Middelburg at 7.30 pm. That meant even tighter time from Middelburg to 702's Sandton studio. Andy Grealey played Nigel Mansell, and when I slid panting into my 702 seat the controller, Thabo Modisane, was playing the jingle for the second time and wondering what next.

The day was expected to become Swaziland's answer to the Boston Tea Party, the Storming of the Bastille, June 16; the beginning of the end for the old regime. In that respect it fell a touch flat, but it was absorbing all right. If ever a country was asking for a revolution, that country is anomalous little Swaziland, the nation of cousins.

Everybody is related to everybody. Everybody professes veneration for the monarchy but is livid at the monarch. 'It's like we're in one man's house,' said an articulate demonstrator. 'One man has all the say and the rest of us are visitors.'

At one point we are peacefully filming a field. It is a pretty field, and a productive one, and is providing visual back-up for a comment I wish to make to the effect that Swaziland has nice things going for it agriculturally. Pretty as it is, this field is not dramatic. Indeed it is the least dramatic thing ever to have our camera focus on it. What we're shooting is, literally, mealies growing.

In the middle of which a friendly Swazi scurries over the road and says: 'You must stop that, or the police will get you.'

I'd think he was mad or joking, except he wasn't the type for either. He explains: there — see, theeeeeeere. Doorengaan in the distance is the back of a big white building.

It's a palace, he says, and the police will zap us if they see a camera. I say that to see the camera from the palace they'd need telescopes. He says that the last lot of journalists who took that line got a long quiet time to reflect upon it.

How the unsuspecting visitor is supposed to detect the back of a palace two miles off is intriguing in its own right. There are palaces all over Swaziland. It must be the world's only country with more royal palaces than it has hospitals, cinemas, railway stations, or airports (say nothing of harbours).

A king is a ridiculous impertinence, rationally, but if you must have one you may as well use it. The Brits use theirs for general welfare. At a royal upkeep of some R500 000 000, it costs each Briton less than two pounds for a year of public entertainment. No wonder the theatres are in trouble.

Swaziland hasn't got the idea yet. Their king still appoints ministers (at least once selecting a new prime minister from a crowd at the royal cattle kraal at Lobamba. 'Who, me?' 'Yes, you, come up here, you're the new head of government.'). He can still tell everybody how long to wear their hair and what colour boots to wear. If you book a flight on Royal Swazi Airlines, hope that the king doesn't decide to commandeer the plane that day. The speed limit halves in the vicinity of palaces, with large threatening roadsigns to say so. Every Swazi will tell you that the royal family 'eat the money'. Swaziland might have been written by Evelyn Waugh. Objectively it is a more oppressive society than South Africa has been since Lord Charles Somerset. But this is oppression of people by their own, and in the eyes of the world that is — not unfairly — lesser oppression.

The king wouldn't see us. The Deputy Prime Minister, Sishayi Nxumalo, was the soul of hospitality.

When I first knew Sishayi, then Simon, he was Minister of Health. Next visit, he was in jail. I saw his wife, who was deeply fearful that he would meet with an accident. The following visit he was a minister again and his former chief jailer, Prince Mfanasabili, was behind bars. Third World Tango. Mfanasibili has had another rise and fall since, and Sishayi is in effect the Grand Vizier. He is the non-Dlamini nice-guy who fronts for the Dlamini regime and disguises the incapacities of whichever Dlamini prince is Prime Minister for the moment. I put it to him that in Swaziland's class system he could only be Deputy or maybe Acting but never Prime, which didn't faze him.

As soon as we'd done he took us all to lunch. While the revolutionaries toyi-toyied outside the Supreme Court fifty yards away, we sat with the nation's de facto chief executive eating prawns in a cramped corner of a Portuguese restaurant. The portly dignified government officials on the far side of our table could only move by tromping across other people's seats. Meantime a constant stream of beggars ambled up to ask for five bob (50c) or cigarettes. They were invariably sent packing in a curt burst of siSwati ack-ack but nobody as much as blinked that they kept on coming.

That's Swaziland. Hectare for hectare it has as much beauty as anywhere in Africa. It is also uncommonly blessed with agriculture, industry, forestry and employment, even if most of this is rather contentiously owned and run by South Africans (and is under strain through the ending of the South African sanctions which did wonders for its growth). With a few twists of the social screw Swaziland could be the jewel of Africa. Then again, with broadly similar twists in every respect except the specific one called the monarchy, there could be plenty of jewels in Africa. The problem is finding how to twist the twists the right way.

16

North West

Some roads, such as the R24 and R27, we saw more of than most. These two lead north west, to places which are far enough from the hub to feel plattelandish but near enough to keep travelling hours to single figures. Handy, when time is tight.

The Treks were not always Treks to a spot on the map. There were Treks into notions too, like the notion 'The Future' and the notion 'Weather'. There were Treks to activities, such as Art and Firefighting and Miss Universe. There were Treks to institutions — the Post Office, the Navy, Hospitals. But Treks to a place had a place too, and Magaliesburg was one such place.

We came, we saw, we reported. I don't know that we reported enough. We met marvellous people such as Oom Steenkamp with a moustache you could make pillows from and a farm you could make a picture-book of, outwardly so engagingly olde worlde that it was a jolt to discover the sophisticated internal reality of the kind of person whose son (Naas) becomes president of the Chamber of Mines.

We touched on good issues. It was new to me to hear farmers say that the crops they farm are no longer dictated by water and soil and climate so much as by which crops can least easily be stolen. We focused on the miracle of Magaliesburg, the eternal spring that bubbles powerfully from Maloney's Eye and bringeth irrigation to the just and the unjust. We revelled in historical fascinations, such as that it was from Maloney's Eye that David Pratt sallied forth one autumn morning to shoot the prime minister, Hendrik Verwoerd. We were absorbed by some less obvious echoes of this event, such as that the farm had been visited afterwards by a series of blights which induced the labourers to persuade the new owner, a man of Italian descent, to let them have the place exorcised by a sangoma. (I wanted to know if the exorcism had helped. The owner said 'I don't believe in that superstitious stuff, I asked the priest to bless the farm and things came right.')

We learned too that the town's oldest farm, quaintly restored as a tea-garden-cum-guesthouse, had once been the site of a para-military invasion. The police suspected it was an ANC base and surrounded the place in mega force. They found no bombs or Umkhonto platoons but they charged the farmer with high treason for spying for the ANC.

Very interesting, I said, I wonder what happened to the farmer.

Oh, I was told, he's a Minister now, Derek Hanekom.

I phoned Derek, Minister of Land Affairs, and he said yes, all true. We arranged to meet at the farm, at 7 am one icy winter morning, and had on camera the kind of heart-warming discussion that is Derek's stock in trade: a combination of rampant humaneness, bucolic love of the land, and earnest desire for a square deal for the undertrodden.

There was also the added element of the personal connection. Derek showed the barn he had built, the field he had cleared, the boiler he had stoked, every so often stopping with an exclamation: 'Gee, this tree has done well!', 'Hullo, Jonas, so you're still here!'

It was a delightful interlude. What is more it showed up fantastically on tape, with sunrise's majestic shadows, the steam blowing visibly from our mouths and nostrils, the spread of frozen dew darkening our boots, the calves in the background frisking for warmth.

It had a sharp end too: a hot ideological fight over land and the landless. For me, the sacrosanctity of private property has moral limits. It has special limits in the case of land, most finite of commodities. When you've got too much of the stuff and you do too little with it, that is where government should swing the jackboot. Some people own lunatic quantities of land, land acquired sometimes by fishy means and sometimes by such distant title that it is crazy for the deeds to remain unassailable, land which sommer sits, useless and unnoticed for generation after generation, while elsewhere Farmer and Peasant fight like wildcats over other land which both want to use. This land, I would *gaps* without a qualm if I were in a state to do so, and I wanted to know why Derek did not look this way for land reform rather than threatening the productive Boer on a thousand hectares with displacement by 500 black families who would all go broke on uneconomic units.

He was taken aback to be attacked from this angle, which, he said, sounded like something he might expect from the wilder quarters of the PAC, but had a ton of reasons why it was not so easy — legal reasons, investor confidence, etc — all very plausible and sensible and wrongful.

After Derek left, we met the local ANC leader, a black guy (who has since become mayor). He invited me to accompany him to ask for an explanation from an Afrikaner who had dragged a petrol jockey 300 metres along a dirt road from his bumper. The transgressor wasn't home. My man left a message with his very polite, if very bewildered, wife: 'I wanted to hear his side of that story. Here's my address. Would you ask him to come and see me.' How's that for forthright local government? (Evidently it turned out that the instant presumption — brute — was cluttered by a complex truth involving, as usual, (a) alcohol and (b) a belief, realistic or not, of being under threat.)

After we left the mayor, we saw a child killed on the main road. A black girl of about ten, she darted from behind a bus and was hit by a Boeretannie in a bakkie. A crowd gathered instantly, about 99% black. Naturally, there were high emotions. I thought this was a set-up to become a racial row and maybe worse than a row. In fact it did the opposite. In a little while the tannie and the mother were hugging each other and crying like sisters. Relatives of both parties arrived, so did police and officials and the school headmaster, and this became an extraordinarily moving experience. There was a general sense of sorrow about the child and for the bereaved, a general sense that the tannie bore no blame and was indeed a victim herself. Grief was common cause, and far from creating racial aggro, the child's death had become an amazing unifier.

So Magaliesburg, aside from a good deal of routine interest, gave us three extremely distinctive episodes. Do you think those three, with their confusions and inaudibilities and major time-consumption, made the screen? Ah, you're learning. We had a fair amount of Hanekom on farm, but not the rest. By my criterion — did we transmit in 28 minutes a reasonable proportion of the impact received in the being there? — Magaliesburg was a bust.

Christa Joubert, SABC3's programme manager, later singled it out as a Trek that didn't go any place much. Dead right, Christa, and paradoxically that is because the crew did too much.

★ ★ ★

The programme on nearby Hartebeespoort suffered from a different problem. We got there by accident to start with. I'd thought we were on our way to see the birth of the new Volkstaat, an as yet unpublicised settlement at Donkerhoek near Pretoria, which I had hoped to combine with a visit to the right-wing Radio Pretoria on adjoining premises. On the night before, I had two messages. There was a polite one from the head of the Volkstaat development to say, sorry, but we feel we must treat this as a private matter, and an execrable one from the head of Radio Pretoria, who spat a Keep Out rejection into my answering machine in a way that might have been designed to reinforce the ugh image that people have of the Righties.

However we were geared up to point northwards and moreover we had a short early morning commercial job near Pretoria that we had allocated for that day in the assumption that we were going there anyway. So we did that job, and then we wandered along the way we happened to be pointed to see what came up.

What came up was Hartebeespoort Dam. We stopped to look around, and I was struck by various features, viz:

- The water, which looks and feels like green paint.

- The commercial precinct, which looks and feels like a prison compound, circa 1930.

- The fact that although the entire metaphor of the town is thick with 'dam', with names of shops and houses playing upon puns of the word, the dam is hidden away. Where it isn't cut off behind high barbed wire, it is obscured behind a high stone wall.

So we began a Trek on Hartebeespoort Dam.

This Trek had fine elements, such as the paragliding. I had assumed that to leap off the top of a mountain with a parachute on your back involved some kind of death wish. When I did it, in tandem with the paragliding association's excellent instructor Jonathan Bass, I discovered that it is more of the opposite —

206

a kind of ultimate peace, and a sport that I have no doubt is headed for major growth over the coming decades.

We also had some fun with the Breakfast Run, the ritual by which the hairiest motorbikes and the ballsiest riders own the R512 on Sunday mornings and speed limits take a weekly walk to oblivion. The riders gather at a restaurant above the dam, where there is a cast-iron pecking order. Every windgat on his Kawasaki has a place, but there is a particular choice place at the top of the hill which is strictly reserved for the very main manne. Unless you're in the 300kph league, or your bike is some sort of legend, or your muscles are Olympian, you stay below.

So we commandeered Shaw Pictures messenger's modest put-a-put bike, complete with delivery box, and I rode to Hartebeespoort. It took me three times as long to get there as it took the real bikies who zoomed past in clouds of dust, their girlfriends turning to stare in disbelief. When I arrived I put-a-putted up to the holy of holies and parked among the Superbikes.

Simon Fourie and a couple of other bike admirals were on hand to provide protection if aggrieved aspirants felt the need to pound me and my tone-lowering iron into the ground. The idea was for the camera to catch the expressions of stupefaction on the faces of the unwitting as I bumbled through the crowd.

We did get some of that, although at moments like this I envy the movie director. The movies have script polished, actors acting to order with prepared expressions at the right time, and lights and cameras and mikes in position. For us it's catch as catch can. Richard and Andrew must just grab whatever they find of real reactions spontaneously expressed, and if Joe or Louis manage to get a mike near the reaction that's a bonus.

The Hartebeespoort Trek had its plus points but it was one of those which left me feeling we hadn't gone far enough. It was too light and scrappy. That was my main worry. A lesser one was the usual sense that I had done someone down; namely

Dries Alberts, a former general secretary of the AWB who had travelled a long and rather nice mental journey into the new SA but whose intelligent perceptions on development and the shortcomings of the town council had been too complex for the cut.

Thus it was a big surprise, the day after the screening, to have a spate of calls from newspapers asking what I felt about the town council's intention to sue me.

I couldn't take this overly seriously. The shopping centre was ugly, the dam did feel like green paint. True, the lady town clerk had given us a lengthy litany of intended and hoped for improvements, and little had featured in the cut, but on that count I felt no guilt. We'd talked to her and her mayor, Piet Rautenbach, for a good twenty minutes, and I had made it clear, as I always do, that twenty minutes on camera routinely shrinks to three or four on screen. In this case the three or four gave, to my mind, a fair but brief hearing to their promises of progress to come. We homed in, naturally, on the most vivid bit, which was an explanation by Rautenbach as to how the algae, or green paint, problem was counteracted by hyacinth, the dam's notorious weed, and how the hyacinth problem stood to be counteracted by hippopotamuses, which would in due course complete the food chain in a benign cycle albeit at the price of certain awkwardnesses for the waterskiers.

Mainly, what upset the council was what was said by one of their two black members — Hartebeespoortdam is one of the rare local authorities with a majority white population. This guy was much less confident of the non-racial brotherhood around the place than his colleagues wanted him to be. He was for instance unhappy that council meetings were in Afrikaans. (I suggested it seemed reasonable that meetings be in the language of the majority. He wondered how happy the whites in the provincial council would be if their meetings were in Tswana.)

Nearly always, the Trek left a good vibe in its wake. We weren't into the business of magnifying animosities, and after a programme was screened we'd usually hear sounds of appreciation — sometimes surprised appreciation — from people who featured.

The Air Force, for instance, had at first said: 'Fine, come along — then submit your tape to us before screening.' I refused, and later, when I was their guest of honour at a thankyou ceremony, I learned that this had plunged them into turmoil. One faction had said: Keep them out or we'll be sorry. The other had said: Take a chance. The Chief of the Air Force plumped for the latter line, with his heart in his boots, he said, and the result was that they were a lot happier afterwards about exposing themselves to the prying eye than they had been before.

At Hartebeespoort, we left dissatisfied customers, and the irony was that they were dissatisfied for reasons utterly remote from my own. I'm sorry whenever there is dissatisfaction, but I'm not losing sleep over this kind of dissatisfaction. I certainly would lose sleep, and plenty, if we were to become a PR exercise.

★ ★ ★

Groot Marico — the third place-Trek to North West — was a better set-up altogether. The programme had quite a lot of the fun-and-games and the local colour. There was a fellow whose party trick, inherited from his father and grandfather before him, is to sing Sarie Marais backwards. We did a midnight wrap under a spectacular moon in the district's main beauty spot, blessed with the eloquent name Die Gat. We danced sokkiejol with the locals. We trotted out the line that if this decrepit one-horse dorp was *Groot* Marico, what could *Klein* Marico be?

We forfeited some good stuff, of course. I would have liked to portray the exchange where I pushed a bunch of sokkiejollers to let me in on the local amusements, and after much humming and hawing they finally proffered the recollection of how the kids used to lay tripwires for the night-soil removers, at the memory of which they all split their sides.

We also missed, through dud tape, a whole discussion with Piet Mampoer. Piet is the town's leading mampoer manufacturer, which therefore means also the world's leading mampoer manufacturer.

He gave us a guided tour of his process and his wares, which at that time and in that place tasted terrific. I wondered vocally why it is that when I go to a Joburg bottle store I am confronted with endless varieties of Russian vodka, Scotch whisky, English gin, American cane, and Jamaican rum, but never oh never a sight of genuine domestic mampoer. I still think that in essence that's a pretty good question. However I also concede that the bottles Piet gave me haven't gone down very much since I got home, where it is somehow less fun to imbibe stuff that blows the top of your head into nuclear fall-out.

The main reason, though, that Marico worked for me is that we went somewhere new — on tape, audibly, cuttably. In fact we went several somewheres new.

For one thing, we went to the school. There has been a spate of coverage of how the Marico, previously the very byword for verkramp and racist, has opened out and now has the model multi-racial school. Yeah? Hmm. True, the miracle by which the old Afrikaans teachers have swung into action teaching the new Tswana pupils is a genuine miracle, and a real heart-booster. Moreover the Tswana kids openly treat having a white teacher as the epitome of privilege and a thing to be striven for, which is an extremely funny turn-up for those of us who remember the former fashion of good riddance to white teachers.

However, alongside the miracle is one vast sham. This is as multi-racial a school as Finland is a multi-racial country. There is one white kid at the school, and he, I happen to know, is there because his parents can't afford the Zeerust bus. There are a tiny handful of Indians and coloureds, and I will take bets that if you care to look in on the 1997 enrolment you will find that this one-time white Group Area has become in effect a black Group Area.

It's not that there is persecution or any such thing; not that there aren't friendships. There are plenty, as far as I could make out. It's just that the non-Africans are foreigners here. The language of the playground is Tswana, and in so far as the language of the blackboard is English it is an English so divided that it might be two languages. We spoke to some senior kids who are close to writing matric in a language in which their conversational skills go barely beyond asking for a Coca Cola and two Chappies. This is not an easy matter to handle, and it is a matter far removed from your standard line of 'hooray, here is the *good* platteland unlike those nasties in Potgietersrus who don't want to let the blacks into their school'. What pleased me was that at least we touched on some of the questions.

In the township later, we had the most honest discussion I have ever heard in respect of the big (I surmise) but publicly undiscussed (that's no surmise) phenomenon of the Africans wondering: what about us?

Marico is a town run by the ANC. Of the ANCs who run the town, one is African. He is not an African who lives in the township where the Africans live; he lives in town where the whites live. A school of township thought does not consider him their representative at all. Some members of that school also allege that in any case he is a councillor without power; the power is in the hands of other ANC councillors, Indians and Afrikaners, whom they do not see as their representatives either. As one of them says: 'The mayor is the richest person in town. On a Saturday morning he can either attend to his shops and make five thousand rands, or he can come here and listen to us telling him that we need a new sewerage pipe or we need the rubbish tip moved. Which do you think he does?'

I listen to these complaints with interest. The nub is that although the councillors are on the council in the name of the party that was voted into power by the Africans, the Africans are out of it.

Being steeped in classical democratic theory, I righteously reply that democracy is not about race, it is about ideology. It is as logical for them to vote for an Indian mayor as it is for, say, Carl Niehaus to vote for an African president. I might as well be talking Greek. They say they never voted for an Indian mayor, they voted for the ANC, because they thought it was the party for the Africans. Now they're out of it once again, on the receiving end while others make the decisions.

Even the most classical of democratic theories revolves around the idea that it is meant to make people feel included. These people do not. Am I to give them a Sociology III lecture, telling them they should not worry because race is merely false consciousness? Nope. I leave gripped by a sense that the great franchise transition, which we leaped with such unexpected smoothness and treated as the millennium, was in truth a small curve on a road whose tricky bits still lie ahead.

From the township we proceed to a church bazaar. An organiser tells me how proud he is that everybody is represented. Everybody? I ask, looking around in vain for a dark complexion. 'Yes,' he says, 'the Hervormdes are here and the Doppers are here and the Apostolics are here, and we go to their bazaars too, these days.'

The bazaar is good & clean & fresh, and as wholesome as can be. Local people are belting out songs (much less of the Sarie Marais than of the Let It Be and Sounds of Silence and Five Hundred Miles). There is a Funny Walks competition. A dominee plays classical guitar. It is relaxed and pleasant and there are jackets left hanging on unattended chairs and there are wallets and car keys lying on unattended tables.

However, something is worrisome. This is an event for the local people, right? Everybody at it will tell me, if I ask, of this or that or another valuable task they are involved in together with their Tswana brothers. They all love Mandela and embrace him as their president. But they perceive 'local people' not a jot less exclusively than their forebears did in the pages of Herman Charles Bosman.

After the bazaar we go to a Volksfees in Swartruggens. This is a much larger activity than the bazaar, and is proud to have collected all the Transvaal's Boere-orkes accordionists under one roof. We as outsiders are given a welcome to make the day feel warmer, the only drawback being that the welcome involves numerous alcoholic beverages in large measures, with the welcomers taking a no-thanks as a rejection.

The Volksfees is quite as white as the bazaar was, but it gives me no pain, and we wrap up the programme with a little reflection on why not. To me, there must always be places for groups to call their own, whether 'group' means whites or Moslems or Afrikaners or nudists or whoever, and no place better than a Volksfees. But if sharing and nationhood are to mean anything at all there must also be places where a stretching occurs, places like town hall functions.

That might not be the most profound observation you heard this year, but it's something, and that's why I look back with fondness upon the Marico programme. Flawed and all, it went new places.

To Be Continued

This was to be a faultless book — rounded, polished, thorough, numerous top-quality photographs excellently reproduced.

We left a few factors out of the calculations. For one, that to deliver top-quality excellently reproduced photographs it is a good idea to first take the photographs.

Trek days, we'd usually start well before dawn as we needed all the daylight we could get.

Starting procedure involved five rules.

1. One person is late.
2. The combi alarm goes off at least twice during loading.
3. Three minutes out of the gate we discover we need petrol.
4. After 50 km someone says: Where's that stills camera?
5. Everyone else says: Oh, shit.

We broke Rule 5 on odd occasions, and someone would say brightly: 'Here it is! In the side-pocket!' Unfortunately, that was where it usually stayed. Video crews and stills photographs are not born for partnership. It was usually up to me to act as reminder-service, and I, too, had other things in mind. None of us are any threat to David Goldblatt, and the camera is the kind you get at the airport chemist shop when they're broadcasting last call for a holiday flight.

We wound up with 64 snapshots of the Kalahari desert and 16 of Andy Grealey and Joe Dlamini poking at the insides of a broken sound system on a KwaZulu hill 300 km from the nearest technician.

Modern technology, its marvels notwithstanding, has not found how to translate Grade A video images to Grade A print images.

Thus, goodbye to the fat coffee-tabler. (Which means hullo to more readers, being a ±R55 book instead of a ±R120 book.)

Then there were those other things — the roundedness, the polishedness and the thoroughness. Well, they're not cancelled, merely delayed. DV there will be 39 more Treks before the end of 1997 and I hope you might care to stoke up your piggy bank in readiness for Trekking II.

★ ★ ★

In farewell, I quote the conclusion of the article on my car in the Karoo:

It is said you choose your friends but not your family. You love your family regardless. But that's only half the point. You don't choose your nation either.

This is my nation. Bullies and gomtorrels and revolutionaries and racists, smiling labourers and selfless samaritans and trusting traders, uprooted swerwers and honest dealers and feudal serfs and dedicated healers, drunks and dimwits and ignoramuses and lost and lonely battlers for survival.

It's still like that.

215